# Pro-Choice? Pro-Life?
# The Questions
# The Answers

by Herbert F. Smith, SJ

ST. PAUL BOOKS & MEDIA

*Nihil Obstat:*
Andrew J. Golias

*Imprimatur:*
✠Anthony Cardinal Bevilacqua
Archbishop of Philadelphia

October 4, 1993

**Library of Congress Cataloging-in-Publication Data**

Smith, Herbert F.
    Pro-choice? pro-life? : the questions, the answers / by
Herbert F. Smith.
       p.    cm.
    ISBN 0-8198-5893-5
    1. Abortion—Moral and ethical aspects. 2. Abortion—
Religious aspects—Catholic Church. 3. Pro-life movement.
4. Pro-choice movement. I. Title.
HQ767.3.S65   1994
363.4'6—dc20                                94-47656
                                                  CIP

Printed and published by Pauline Books & Media, 50 St. Paul's
Avenue, Boston, MA 02130.

Pauline Books & Media is the publishing house of the Daughters
of St. Paul, an international congregation of women religious
serving the Church with the communications media.

1 2 3 4 5 6 7 8 9                            99 98 97 96 95

# Contents

**1. With all the problems in the world, and all of us due to die anyway, is it right to upset society over the abortion issue the way pro-life people do?**

We make a great stir about right-to-human-life because it is such an "inestimable gift" that we feel the obligation to protect the rights of every new human life, and respect the rights of its Creator to whom we are responsible.

A Russian proverb states: "Nothing is worth the life of an innocent child." The bishops of the Second Vatican Council reflected a similar idea when they said that "abortion and infanticide are unspeakable crimes."[1]

Since "Charity begins at home," consider an effect of legalized abortion that directly threatens us all. The moment the law deprives one category of human beings of equality with other human beings, the dignity and rights of all human beings are threatened. Our Founding Fathers tried to ward off that threat by declaring: "We hold these truths to be self-evident, that all men are created equal, that they are endowed by their Creator with certain unalienable Rights, that among these are Life, Liberty and the pursuit of Happiness."

The threat has ripened into danger for the aged. In 1992, a euthanasia bill in California got much support, though in the end strenuous leadership by the Church helped fellow Christians and other concerned people defeat it—this time.

Abortion threatens our sense of the meaning of life. Many people have lost a sense of life's value, and are adrift. Some are suicidal. The Congregation for the Doctrine of the Faith defines life's meaning: "From the moment of conception, the life of every human being is to be respected in an absolute way because man is the only creature on earth that God has 'wished for himself' and the spiritual soul of each man is 'immediately created' by God; his whole being bears the imprint of the Creator. Human life is sacred because from its beginning it involves 'the creative action of God,' and it remains forever in a special relationship with the Creator, who is its sole end. God alone is the Lord of life from its beginning until its end: No one can in any circumstance claim for himself the right to destroy directly an innocent human being."[2]

The Congregation speaks of the "inestimable value" of this gift of life as the foundation on which to base such reflections as those being made here.

Finally, if the lives we were protecting were our own or those of our loved ones, would we think any stir too great?

## 2. Isn't right to life predominately a Catholic issue?

The facts ring out *No!* When the controversy began to rage even more fiercely after the infamous *Roe v. Wade* Supreme Court decision legalized abortion, the moral rejection of the decision was ascribed to Catholics. But in fact we were never alone. Admittedly, Catholics were the first to mount a concerted outcry.

There's an interesting story about this. A small commune of non-Catholics in California, founded to preserve family values, was shocked by *Roe v. Wade*. They agreed to identify any Church standing foursquare against abortion as the true Church. The evidence led them to the Catholic Church. Against their earlier inclinations—the group included Jews and Protestants—they converted to Catholicism. They formed a third order, the St. Martin de Porres Dominican Community, to live like the early Christians, and share their belongings. They also founded "Catholics United for Life," to uphold the right to life and to teach chastity.

Moral goodness and moral evil cut across all boundaries, and many other Christians and people of other religions and no religion have come through in ways that shame many a Catholic. Two instances will suffice.

*The Catholic League Newsletter* carried an article entitled, "'Catholic Issue' myth exploded." It reports that the Christian Action Council, the nation's largest Protestant pro-life group, tabulated the following vote on the pro-life Hyde Amendment in the House of Representatives: Baptists: 24 in favor, 19 against; Episcopalians: 28 in favor, 23 opposed; Lutherans: 12 in favor, 3 opposed; Presbyterians: 31 in favor, 18 opposed; Catholics: 80 in favor, 31 opposed.

The article also quotes the Council's Executive Director as saying that Protestants, "in rapidly increasing numbers," are opposing abortion regardless of the position of their denomination's leadership.[3]

Another Catholic paper reported the remarkable *Durham Declaration*, produced by a group of prominent United Methodist bishops, pastors, and theologians. It admits: "Abortion is testing our Church today as deeply as slavery tested our Church in the 19th Century . . . stirring up great confusion . . . ." It adds: "We confess that we have often compromised the Gospel by submitting to the seductions of society. We have exchanged the message of salvation in Jesus Christ for a false message about human potential." The declaration then refers to our culture's claim that we have a right to do with our bodies what we want, and states: "We United Methodists declare that this is false."

And then, loud and clear: "We pledge, with God's help, to teach our churches that the unborn child is created in the image of God and is one for whom the Son of God died. This child is God's child. So the life of this child is not ours to take. Therefore, it is sin to take this child's life for reasons whether of birth control, gender selection, convenience or avoidance of embarrassment."[4]

### 3. At any rate, isn't right to life just a religious issue?

It is not, though the media still tend to insinuate that it is. Few issues that believers call to the attention of society are simply religious in nature. Most are social issues in their own right. "You shall not kill" is a divine commandment, taught by all the churches, but even atheist countries forbid murder. Few people want that law changed!

The right to life issue fits in here. It fits whether one holds that the newly conceived human being is at once a person, or simply the beginnings of human life. It is the life of the next generation of society. Even the infamous *Roe v. Wade* decision admitted that society has a stake in life in the womb. It allowed some [grossly inadequate] rights to states to protect the unborn baby in its latest stages of gestation.

In *The Church, Public Policy & Abortion*, The Pennsylvania bishops affirmed: "We address this issue of abor-

tion not as a narrow sectarian concern but as a fundamental human issue that touches every person of any or
no creed."

We can bring this home by asking a question: If
abortion could be applied retroactively, to affect ourselves, would atheists still favor abortion?

In their 1968 letter, *Human Life in Our Day*, the
American Catholic bishops wrote: "It is becoming clear
that the believer and the humanist alike have common
concerns for both life and peace." They quote an agnostic
philosopher, Eric Fromm, who demands to know: "Why
do not those who represent the traditions of religion and
humanism speak up and say that there is no deadlier sin
than love for death and contempt for life?" Fromm calls
us "to arouse and stimulate love for life as opposed to
love for gadgets."

When Nazi Germany murdered millions of Jews,
and used others for human experiments, was it solely a
Jewish question? Or was it solely a German question
because Germans perpetrated it? It was a human issue,
and the war crimes trial treated it as such.

Jewish Dr. Bernard Nathanson, who founded the
National Abortion Rights Action League and ran abortion clinics himself, has converted to the pro-life position. He has produced the leading pro-life video, *The
Silent Scream*. He now proclaims that abortion is the new
holocaust.

With over a million U.S. babies killed a year, is it
a religious issue because believers are in the forefront of
the battle to stop the carnage? Is it a religious issue
even though many of the victims are the babies of non-
believers?

Clearly, since the victims are human, it is a human
issue. Since they are being deprived of life and limb
without accusation or trial, it is a human rights issue.

To call abortion a religious issue is simply inaccurate. Lincoln is supposed to have asked: "If you call a donkey's tail a leg, how many legs does the donkey have?" The answer is: four, because calling a tail a leg doesn't make it one. Abortion is an issue for all humans, believers and non-believers, because it is a human issue. For a believer it is a human issue with strong religious content.

Religion doesn't belong only to members of revealed faiths like Christianity, Judaism and Islam. God can be known from reason, and philosophy studies the question of God in the branch called natural theology. Nor does the fact that Catholics believe God infuses an immortal soul into the new human life in the womb make it only a Catholic or Christian question. The precise moment God does this is not definitively disclosed in Christian revelation. Efforts to determine the moment from experimental knowledge go on among Catholic theologians. But any philosopher who has come to a knowledge of God by human reason can also ponder this question. Since secular universities teach philosophy, this matter falls within their purview as well. Thus the religious question and questions concerning the occupant of the womb impose themselves on every human being who is open to thought.

Human life in every stage is a human issue, a social issue, a religious issue. Bodily life here below is the fundamental social human right without which all other rights are zeros.

### 4. Do you deny that religion is an important factor in the pro-life camp?

Not at all. The pro-choice arguments can be very persuasive. We need all the help we can get to see aright, especially when the pro-life arguments are suppressed, as the media often does. It is true that when people weigh both the serious pro-choice arguments and the pro-life arguments, those who decide in favor of pro-life are more likely to act accordingly if they are believers. For while all have the motive of acting according to what is right, believers are reinforced by their duty to God. Further, the pro-life arguments from reason are often reinforced by others from revelation. These advantages prevail in many matters of human conduct.

The Pennsylvania Catholic bishops, in their 1990 statement, *The Church, Public Policy & Abortion*, quote from George Washington's farewell address as follows:

"Of all the dispositions and habits which lead to political prosperity, religion and morality are indispensable supports . . . . And let us with caution indulge the supposition that morality can be maintained without religion. Whatever may be conceded to the influence of refined education on minds of peculiar structure, reason and experience both forbid us to expect that national morality can prevail in exclusion of religious principles."

While the Judeo-Christian basis of our U.S. culture prevailed, even non-believers were immersed in it and formed by it. But that basis has been thrown out bit by bit in recent decades. In 1992, William Barr, then Attorney General, observed: "Moral tradition has given way to moral relativism." He saw the results as alarming, and quoted John Adams: "We have no government armed with power which is capable of contending with human passions unbridled by morality and religion. Our Constitution was made only for a moral and religious people, it is wholly inadequate for the government of any other."

Barr concludes that "the framers viewed themselves as launching a great experiment." In Barr's judgment, the loss of a shared public philosophy endangers our whole way of life, and family life disintegrates.[5] Without a strongly religious people, it is unlikely that endangered babies would have a chance to survive.

## 5. Then you admit there is strength in the pro-choice arguments?

They have great persuasive force. Our pro-life stand feels that force and anguishes over it. Family and maternal suffering are often very great. Unless we hold to truth, to responsibility, to the compact with life, to compassion for the unborn children, to the natural law that speaks to conscience, and to higher and absolute values and the law of God that claims mind and heart, we will yield to our feelings and emotions. But these are not the sole bases for judgment and action. Judgment is often impaired because the media lopsidedly give us the case for pro-choice, not the case for pro-life with the moral arguments presented here.

No one has put the pro-choice arguments more compellingly than The Sacred Congregation for the Doctrine of the Faith in its 1974 *Declaration on Procured Abortion*:

"Divine law and natural reason . . . exclude all right to the direct killing of an innocent person. However, if the reasons given to justify an abortion were always manifestly evil and valueless, the problem would not be so dramatic. The gravity of the problem comes from the fact that in certain cases, perhaps in quite a considerable number of cases, by denying abortion one endangers important values to which it is normal to attach great value, and which may sometimes even seem to have priority. We do not deny these very great difficulties. It may be a serious question of health, sometimes of life or death, for the mother; it may be the burden represented by an additional child, especially if there are good reasons to fear that the child will be abnormal or retarded; it may be the importance attributed in different classes of society to considerations of honor or dishonor, of loss of social standing, and so forth" (n. 14).

Why, then, does the Congregation still uphold the evil of abortion? Because, as the quote says at the beginning, "Divine law and natural reason . . . exclude all right to the killing of an innocent person." And so the statement continues: "We proclaim only that none of these reasons can ever objectively confer the right to dispose of another's life, even when that life is only beginning." Don't we grant this in the case of any other human life? Then why discriminate against babies?

If babies had a voice to tell their woes, wouldn't we hear the persuasive arguments in favor of abortion outweighed by more powerful ones against it? They are summarized in an application of the Fifth Commandment: "You shall not kill us!"

One of the greatest strengths of the pro-choice position is the use of the phrase *pro-choice*, for we all value freedom to choose. But consider what David Boldt, an editor of the *Philadelphia Inquirer*, who insists he is undecided, has to say: "One clear sign that even people who want to keep abortion legal are made uncomfortable by it is the widespread use of the term *pro-choice*, easily the most fatuous euphemism ever to creep into the American political lexicon."[6] His point is that what we are dealing with is not some neutral issue of "choosing" but the issue of deciding whether or not to maintain the legal right to kill unborn human life.

Our opponents charge that pro-life people take a similar advantage: by calling ourselves *pro-life* we imply that others are not. That's why the media rarely label us anything but anti-abortion, while regularly calling the pro-choice people by their chosen term. But even if our term also carries a favorable bias, consider this: Anti-abortion means "against expelling the human fetus," that is, against killing a developing human being. The term pro-choice, on the other hand, avoids the topic to

which it refers. Would pro-choice people agree to call
themselves pro-abortionists if we pro-life people agreed
to settle for the term anti-abortionists? It would make for
a more honest exchange.

Many pro-choice people agree that the killing of
4,000[7] unborn U.S. children a day is no really human
way to relieve the suffering of women and families. That
means the death of more than one million, four hundred
thousand children a year—more than all the deaths of all
the soldiers in all American wars together.[8] Shouldn't we
alleviate the suffering not by war on the unborn, but by
directly relieving the problems that cause it? One feminist said, "No one is in favor of abortion." She was
pleading for a better solution.

## 6. What special knowledge does the Catholic Church claim, to address herself to non-members and non-believers?

The last two answers comprise a partial response.
Many questions that the Church deals with are at root
human issues which reflect the natural law embedded in
the human heart, whether or not one believes in the God
who embedded them. That is why, in social matters,
even atheistic communism concurred with the Church
on some points.

Further, Church spokespersons are learned people
who have as much right to address social issues as other
commentators. Even when it does not teach in terms of
revelation, the Church often expresses these issues very
clearly. It has the help of the Holy Spirit and of its great
saints and sages. It has gathered the wisdom of thinkers
from all ages, even from the ancients.

In a debate with an Orthodox bishop, one atheist
admitted that he looked into the teaching of the

churches, if only to judge whether he was out on a limb or worse.

Pope Paul VI answered our question when, at the U.N., he described the Church as "an expert in humanity." Her role, he said elsewhere, is to foster "the civilization of love."[9]

Further, the Church reminds believers, and calls unbelievers, to heed the truth that we cannot toy with human life, because it is a direct work of God: "That souls are immediately created by God," Pius XII taught, "is a view which the Catholic faith imposes on us."[10]

## 7. What's the basic issue between pro-choice and pro-life people?

The basic issue is very basic: Is innocent human life sacred, or is it moral to allow it to be destroyed legally? Must society protect life, or should it let individuals decide the question themselves? Another question lurks here: Can a society that doesn't protect human life survive?

Ancient Roman society had such a severe problem with abortion and infanticide that it required couples who wished to wed to swear before many witnesses that they would bear children. That society was concerned for its own future. One commentator has pointed out that the only real social security is children. What good is paper money or even gold bullion if there are no young to work when the old retire? Some western nations thinned by abortion are already importing people.

Another basic issue is whether we can ever have civil peace in a society that legalizes abortion. Earnest pro-life people can find no rest of soul in an abortionist society. The law of love that binds all human beings together impels them to feel an unescapable responsibility to work and struggle until the wrong against the unborn is righted. "Nor shall you stand by idly," the Scriptures say, "when your neighbor's life is at stake" (Lev 19:16).* We all instinctively feel this truth where the issue comes to sharpest focus.

## 8. How answer the objection that pro-life people want the government to deny women the right to control their own bodies?

In support of the common good, the government may restrict our control of our bodies. It forbids such things as prostitution and non-medical use of addictive drugs.

The objection is an emotional, not a factual one. Put more frankly, the objection is: "You deny me the right to kill the occupant of my womb, even though it is more of a burden than I want to bear." The issue is one of two lives, not one. The burden of pregnancy can be great for women who don't want a child, but it doesn't justify the killing of innocent life. All of us should work together to ease a distressed mother's burden through programs of care and adoption, but we cannot approve of killing, or be silent about it.

In truth, the abortion issue arises because men and women fail to control their bodies in sexually responsible ways. Don't we all wish that people would control their bodies so these grave confrontations would not arise in society?

## 9. Doesn't it seem hard and unfair that an unmarried woman is often burdened with the whole responsibility of bearing and supporting a child when the man involved often escapes completely?

It is hard and unfair. A truly just and human society would not condone sexual laxity and permissiveness. It would not promote such things as the use for profit of sexually suggestive advertisements that lead to so many out-of-wedlock pregnancies. A sane society would not fail to train its children in the responsibilities of life and of sexuality that have always been seen as necessary to prevent the tragedy of unwed mothers.

It is clearly the law of nature and nature's God that sexual activity is oriented to conception and responsibility for the child conceived. For either the father or the mother to shun responsibility for a child conceived leads only to further grief for both.

No man who fathers a child and abandons both mother and child can have any respect for himself. This too is the law of nature and of nature's God. The Catholic Church certainly teaches that a father is responsible for his child, whether he fathers it in or out of wedlock. Once a child is conceived, it has the right to life. The rights and duties of child and parents are complementary and reconcilable. Must we not all do all we can to make these truths more forcefully present in our Church and our culture? Can any of us divorce ourselves from the task?

A single, pregnant woman who needs help beyond that her family can or will give her can find it wherever pro-life activity and responsible government exist. In fact many organizations, like Birthright, have sprung up to provide that help. Most Catholic dioceses have a Family Life Office which helps needy pregnant women. Services provided include pregnancy testing, counseling, pre-natal and post-natal care, housing, family support, and adoption programs. The woman can choose among these resources. Pro-life centers also guide women to the many services which government provides.

What is the right attitude toward a pregnant single girl or woman? Put the question another way: How can we relate to her according to the Heart of Christ? In a disordered society like ours, we should honor a pregnant single woman who resists the abortion culture, and has the courage to bear her child.

Whatever the woman did wrong, she is doing something good now. She needs our love, understanding and care. Is it right to drive a human being to "correct" an act of passion by committing an act of abortion?

Whatever her fault may have been, to accept her now is not to approve of any fault, any more than God approves of sin when he forgives and rescues us. We remember how kindly Jesus treated the woman charged with adultery, and we imitate him. We should make it clear to a pregnant woman that we think she is acting bravely if she bears her child. She pleases God very much, and atones for any weakness in the past. We should be willing to help her bring her child into the world.

**10. Still, if you agree that a woman has a right to control her own body, aren't you in conflict with yourself when you say she has no right to an abortion?**

No. Are there any rights that don't entail corresponding obligations? None of us has a right to use or refuse use of our bodies regardless of our obligations. Our bodies belong not only to ourselves, but in varying degrees to our God, our spouses, our children, our nation.

TO GOD: God holds Author's rights over our bodies. He has expressed the basics in the Ten Commandments. "You shall not commit adultery" puts a limit on the use of our bodies. "You shall not kill" forbids killing any other human being in or out of the womb. The Christian is even more explicitly told, "Do you not know that your body is a temple of the Holy Spirit within you, which you have from God? You are not your own" (1 Cor 6:19).

TO ONE'S SPOUSE: Married lovers instinctively accept St. Paul's words: "The husband should give to his wife her conjugal rights, and likewise the wife to her husband. For the wife does not rule over her own body, but the husband does; likewise the husband does not rule over his own body, but the wife does" (1 Cor 7:3-4).

A woman who denies her husband his rights and duties toward a child they conceived undermines her marriage. Even if a woman is not married to the father of the child, he still shares rights and duties toward the child with her.

TO ONE'S CHILDREN: Nature and nature's God make the natural use of sex simultaneously love-giving and life-giving. To use sex responsibly is to take responsibility for the new human life generated. Recall that abortion casts a human being from the life-sustaining maternal home ordained for him or her by nature and nature's God. The child in the womb is often torn limb from limb in the process, because it refuses to go easily "into that dark night."

TO ONE'S FELLOW CITIZENS AND NATION: A nation's security requires that soldiers expose their bodies to danger and death. Cowardice and treason are punished by disgrace and even death.

Women have by nature a special call to loyalty to life and its nurture. Abortion is a kind of treason to the human race. This sense of feminine loyalty to life is beautifully captured in a statue in Valley Forge National Park. Among the remembrances of men who died for their country in the revolution is a noble statue of a woman who gave her life in childbirth.

TO REASON ITSELF: Reason acknowledges the foregoing truths. Rights and obligations are partners. Our right to use our bodies is limited by the effects our actions have on ourselves and others. To deny sane limits is lawlessness, and even a departure from rational conduct. The fact that a child is in its mother's body gives her a responsibility to care for it, not a right to kill it.

The nationally known pro-life activist Molly Kelly asks this question: If a woman were transparent so she could see the baby within, would any woman have an abortion?

Many feminists have made the trek from a pro-choice stance to a pro-life one. Feminist Frederica Mathewes-Green describes how she bought the slogan, "Don't labor under a misconception—legalize abortion." By a slow path she came to see that "we have let in a Trojan horse whose hidden betrayal we've just begun to see."

She points out that, for more than 100 years, earlier feminists warned against abortion as violence and oppression against women. She recalls how women like Susan B. Anthony, Elizabeth Cady Stanton, and Emma Goldman called it violence and oppression against women and children, child murder, proof of the misery of the working class, and barbaric. Simone de Beauvoir termed it "a disowning of feminine values." Mathewes-Green concludes by saying that to look with contempt on childbearing "is to reject our distinctive power, our bodies, ourselves.'"[11]

It's not we opponents of abortion who are in conflict with ourselves, but the women who choose abortion. By abortion a woman attacks not only her offspring but her body's natural way of functioning. She is in conflict with herself as an embodied person. That's easy to see, and it expresses what religion means when it affirms that sin is against reason.

## 11. The Supreme Court's **Roe v. Wade** decision legalized abortion. Must we not respect human law, as even Scripture says?

St. Thomas Aquinas defines law as "an ordination of reason" promulgated for the good of society by those in charge. A law that defies reason and rebels against the natural law and the law of God harms persons and society and must be resisted and changed rather than obeyed. Even the ancient pagans knew that.

Some 400 years before Christ, Sophocles wrote his drama, *Antigone*. The king forbade Antigone to fulfill the sacred duty of burying her brother, because he had been killed fighting against his own city. When she did so anyway she was hailed before the king who challenged her boldness. She replied that his law was not in accord with the "justice of the gods"; that his law had no right to override the unwritten, immutable laws of heaven, good for all time, "and no man knows when they were first put forth."[12]

After the Second World War, the war crimes trials upheld the responsibility to adhere to truths that are above human law. The defense that they acted under orders did not exonerate those guilty of atrocities in the holocaust.

Pope John Paul II refers to *Antigone* in a footnote in his Exhortation *On Reconciliation and Penance in the Mission of the Church Today*. He attaches the footnote to the passage where he says: "People cannot come to true and genuine repentance until they realize that sin is contrary to the ethical norm written in their inmost being" (n. 31).

The American Revolution began when good people rebelled against unjust English laws. Ages before, when St. Peter and St. John were on trial for carrying out Christ's mandate they declared: "Whether it is right in the sight of God for us to obey you rather than God, you be the judges" (Acts 4:19).

The Sacred Congregation for the Doctrine of the Faith's 1974 *Declaration on Procured Abortion* states expressly: "Human law can abstain from punishment, but it cannot declare to be right what would be opposed to the natural law, for this opposition suffices to give the assurance that a law is not a law at all.

"It must in any case be clearly understood that whatever may be laid down by civil law in this matter [of abortion], man can never obey a law which is in itself immoral, and such is the case of a law which would admit in principle the liceity of abortion" (nn. 21, 22). The Declaration says that we must both resist such laws and work to change them.

Mahatma Gandhi did that in a parallel case. When on trial for civil disobedience against British rule, he said, "I am here . . . to invite and submit to the highest penalty that can be inflicted on me for what in law is a deliberate crime and what appears to me to be the highest duty of a citizen." He told his judge he should either inflict the due punishment, or resign so as not to support an evil system of laws.

More than one American has done just that. A former Fraternal Order of Police President resigned as a public candidate for Philadelphia Sheriff because he could not morally carry out the duty of jailing abortion protesters.[13]

Dissenting judges and other legal experts have observed that the *Roe v. Wade* decision struck down the state laws against abortion on no sound basis of Constitution or precedent. It seems there was a good case for impeachment.

Judge John T. Noonan, Jr.'s book, *A Private Choice*, is an excellent source to answer our question about the respect due the Supreme Court's abortion decision: The

Court lacked the right to hand down such a decision. Noonan says that in 1789, when the original articles of the Constitution were adopted, the English jurist Sir William Blackstone "was the bible of the American lawyers, and Blackstone taught that a 'person' was 'one like us' who had been 'formed by God' in the womb."

Noonan adds that "abortion, though not widely practiced because of medical difficulties in doing it safely, was a crime at common law if the pregnancy had reached the stage where movements by the child were perceptible; and if the child in the womb was injured by an abortifacient, was born alive, and died from his injury, the crime was murder." He continues: "the articles gave the new government no power to disturb the administration of the common laws by the states." He then shows that the pertinent later amendments to the Constitution further supported the child in the womb, until in fact some states "made abortion a crime from conception."[14]

*Webster's Ninth New Collegiate Dictionary* defines *common law* as "the body of law developed in England primarily from judicial decisions based on custom and precedent, unwritten in statute or code, and constituting the basis of the English legal system and of the system in all of the U.S. except Louisiana." Crucial here is that common law is a legal tradition that developed out of the hearts of the citizens, and was commonly accepted even by judges.

In a chapter which examines expert opinion on the legal foundations for the Court's decision, Judge Noonan says: "The balance of expert opinion viewed the liberty [to have an abortion] as a disaster" and "the weight of their judgment was overwhelming." The experts concluded that the Court's decision was "without principle, a failure; a refusal of the Court's own discipline, a transgression of all limits, something that will not do; naked political preference, comprehensive legislation . . . ." Noonan concludes: "Scholarly authority judged the liberty to lack constitutional basis. Its establishment, Justice [Byron] White had said, was an act of raw judicial power. If the liberty did not have a foundation in the Constitution or in constitutional principle, its basis had to lie in politics" (p. 32).

In plain English, for political reasons the Court usurped the prerogative of the Congress to make laws. It usurped the right of the people to elect their lawmakers, and to replace them at the next election if they don't like the laws they make.

Our abortion law is in conflict with the United Nations' *Declaration on the Rights of the Child* approved by the General Assembly on November 20, 1959. It states that "the child, owing to his physical and intellectual immaturity, needs particular attention and special care, including adequate medical protection, both before and after birth."[15] Clearly implied here is the right to be born.

After the Supreme Court's infamous *Dred Scott* decision which denied citizenship to blacks, Lincoln was asked if the founding fathers meant to include blacks as equal to whites in the "unalienable right to life, liberty, and the pursuit of happiness." His answer: "This they said, and this they meant."[16]

Is there any reason to think they didn't include babies? The Pennsylvania Pro-Life Federation of Pittsburgh put out a publication, "Changed Role of Physician Reveals Extent of Abortion Crisis." In it they quote an 1871 statement of the American Medical Association. In part, the statement reads: "We shall discover an enemy in the camp; men who cling to a noble profession only to dishonor it; men who seek not to save, but to destroy; men known as abortionists. . . . The abortionists are more destructive to human life than ten British armies. . . ." Reference to the British reminds us that people in 1871 were much closer to the Founding Fathers than we are, and felt more deeply what the Revolution was all about.

The statesman Alexander Hamilton participated in the founding of our nation. He published a pamphlet in 1775 called *The Farmer Refuted*. In it, he defended the same four truths of natural law which the Declaration of Independence included a year later as the foundation for the new nation: "Good and wise men, in all ages . . . have supposed that the deity . . . has constituted an eternal and immutable law, which is indispensibly obligatory upon all mankind, prior to any human institution whatsoever. This is what is called the law of nature, 'which being coeval with mankind, and dictated by God himself, is, of course, superior in obligation to any other . . . no human laws are of any validity if contrary to this . . .'" (Blackstone).[17]

Malcolm Muggeridge, speaking of the holocaust, compared it with the slaughter of some fifty million preborn children a year in the world. He observed: "You can say that in our mad world, it takes about thirty years to transform a war crime into a compassionate act."[18]

It is because we respect human law that we cry out against lawless law. Professor Noonan's book, cited above, reminds us that the Supreme Court has reversed itself in the past, and could do so regarding abortion. Four times in the past, constitutional amendments reversed bad decisions. We must work for an amendment now; and he advises how to do it (p. 178-188).

To conclude, then: It's evident we cannot obey immoral laws. The Book of Ecclesiastes says: "Moreover I saw under the sun that in the place of justice, even there was wickedness, and in the place of righteousness, even there was wickedness" (3:16). When we see the same, we must work in every honest way to restore justice.

## 12. Can it be a legal and moral good to extend civil disobedience in favor of the unborn to disturbing the peace by obstructing abortion clinics, destroying property, and burning down abortion facilities?

Is it legal? For the most part, no. Is it commendable? No official Church document this author has read advocates it. Is it morally permissible or desirable? That is a complex and difficult question. No answer can cover all cases. The best that can be done in a brief space is to offer some analysis and guidelines.

The moral and legal question here is: To what lengths can one go to resist an unjust aggressor? The answer: One can resist only to the degree necessary, and only in a way proportioned to the harm being done.

A simple example will help. If a thief is stealing a lawn mower from a yard, an owner who shot him dead would be morally and legally guilty of homicide. A shout could probably scare the thief away, and safeguard one's property. But even if the thief tried to throw the lawn mower into a car and drive away, to shoot him would be murderous. No lawn mower is worth a person's life.

An abortion clinic entails a far more serious matter. It is an unjust aggressor against human life, as is the society which legalizes abortion. In principle, it is not excessive force to destroy property to safeguard human life. For example, a person could break into a house to save someone being violently attacked, even if extensive property damage resulted.

As to overturning public peace, it is the abortionists and the lawmakers who have overturned it. "They have healed the wound of my people lightly, saying, 'Peace, peace,' when there is no peace. Were they ashamed when they committed abomination? No, they were not at all ashamed; they did not know how to blush"

(Jer 6:14-15). Pro-life tactics can be attempts to restore true peace by awakening the public conscience.

Are these tactics desirable and commendable, then? That is the critical question. Do they advance the cause of the unborn, or stir such charges of fanaticism against pro-life people, however unjustly, that they do more harm than good for the cause of life? If so, is it because such tactics are not truly Christian?

Envision a parallel case to bring out the point. An ardent pro-life legislator is faced with a constitutional amendment that would forbid all abortions except in the case of rape and incest. Passage will save millions of unborn babies. Failure to pass it because it still contains a grave injustice will sacrifice millions of lives to principle. Since "politics is the art of the possible," he or she votes for the bill, convinced it's the moral thing to do in the circumstances. One hopes that when sanity is restored, rape and incest abortions will be voted out too. Catholic moral principles accept this decision as morally valid.

Applying this lesson, we ask these questions: Will violent tactics save a few babies at the cost of hardening public sentiment against pro-life people, and thus cost many more unborn lives in the end? Or will such actions penetrate consciences not sensitive to the evil of killing human life in the womb?

It would be unwise simply to deny the truly pro-phetic action that may be involved here. God does stir people to heroic prophetic actions. But is this one of them? Not every prophet is a true prophet. People who sincerely think they are acting prophetically can be sin-cerely wrong. How often does violence serve the cause against violence? One cannot help but recall the Sermon on the Mount, the turning of the other cheek, and Christ as the Man of Peace.

These points don't touch all the major issues here. Often, pro-life people who use any sort of violence target

clinics that perform third-trimester abortions, where the
unborn children are so advanced in their development
that no reasonable person can deny that murder is taking
place. How much does that change the issue?

But anyone who would practice this form of civil
disobedience owes it to both the unborn children and the
whole pro-life movement to ponder carefully whether it
will do more harm than good. "The science of the saints
is prudence."

Are Operation Rescue Workers prudent? Prudence
is the virtue of practical reason which directs human
actions in accordance with truth. Besides that, a divinely
infused virtue of prudence regulates all our actions
through charity. The gift of counsel goes still further and
makes us especially docile to the guidance of the Holy
Spirit of Love.

A *Wall Street Journal* editorial had something pertinent to say about Operation Rescue. It pointed out in
1991 that more than 40,000 arrests had been made outside abortion clinics, and that Operation Rescue had
stirred much outrage.

Then it reminded us that civil disobedience cam-
paigns don't require majority support—only success: A
Gallup poll after the 1963 Birmingham march found that
60% of respondents thought such demonstrations hurt
civil rights. "Yet within months, the marchers had ob-
tained their main objective: the passage of the Civil
Rights Act."[19]

We have to reflect carefully on how our Pastors
assess any form of violence in pro-life work. Anthony
Cardinal Bevilacqua addressed this whole issue after
Operation Rescue had scheduled activities in the Philadelphia archdiocese. "I believe the best answer about
what type of protest is most appropriate comes through
prayerful examination of individual conscience" he said.
He praised Birthright, referred to counseling, adoption

services, and "prayerful and peaceful demonstrations outside of abortion clinics." Then he added, "Some, like Operation Rescue volunteers, have chosen civil disobedience. While actions of civil disobedience are matters of personal conscience, we must always remember that violence to others can never be justified." He also pointed out that the advent of RU-486 abortion pills will push the abortion process more and more into the private sector, where the only effective pro-life policy will be to change hearts.[20]

This author certainly agrees that the way of Christ is the way of patience and long-suffering in the service of peace, which the Church teaches. But the Church has long since accepted passive resistance to evil laws and deeds, and that acceptance stands. Beyond that, violence, even when it is morally justifiable, can only be allowed as a matter of last resort.

In today's highly-charged climate concerning abortion, it is important for pro-lifers to avoid any type of violent activity. Violence contradicts the pro-life message completely.

Cardinal Bernard Law of Boston has stated: "If we are to root ourselves effectively in the way of non-violence, it is essential to recognize that violence has its beginning in a turning from God and a turning from our neighbor. That vision of human solidarity which flows from Christ's teaching is foreign to the violent heart. Jesus said that we would be known as his disciples by the love we show one another. . . . Any demonstration characterized by violence would, of its very nature, be out of order. . . . The pro-life message cannot be heard in the midst of violence, whether that violence be in thought, word or deed" (*The Pilot*, January 6, 1995).

In conclusion, then: In all pro-life activity, charity must extend to those who have abortions, those who perform them, and lawmakers who pass the laws that permit them. Will our action harden them, or convert them? Will the outcry it generates discourage good pro-life workers and make them feel like giving up? Only when we consider everyone we influence will we act most wisely, and do the most good for the unborn.

### 13. You've been calling abortion killing, but how call it murder or even serious sin until science determines when life begins?

Science has its part to play in decisions about human life and its beginnings. But medical science draws conclusions that are repeatedly revised, especially with regard to the origins and stages of human life. Still, churchmen, theologians, philosophers, and everyone else must integrate scientific knowledge into the web of moral decision making.

It is instructive to remember that people had to make decisions in this matter before there was any modern science. They used experience, observation, and common sense, plus the judgments of the wise of every age. Their judgments continued to be affirmed in most matters until modern culture attacked them, generally not for any scientific reasons. In fact, modern scientific knowledge concerning the first stages of human life supports the traditional moral positions far more than did the erroneous biological information available to Aristotle and St. Thomas Aquinas.

Through the ages, as in the Scriptures, a pregnant woman would say, "I am with child." And even in our culture today friends commonly ask a pregnant woman, "How is the baby?"

The Second Vatican Council, following unvarying tradition, taught that "life once conceived, must be protected with the utmost care; abortion and infanticide are abominable crimes."[21] More recently, the Holy See confirmed in its *Charter of the Rights of the Family* that "human life must be absolutely respected and protected from the moment of conception."

The Congregation for the Doctrine of the Faith's 1987 "Instruction on Respect for Human Life in Its Origin and on the Dignity of Procreation" (*Donum Vitae*) quotes and footnotes these Vatican II texts (I, 1), and adds that "From the time that the ovum is fertilized, a new life is begun which is neither that of the father nor of the mother; it is rather the life of a new human being with his own growth. It would never be made human if it were not human already" (I, 1).

The document goes on to consider the then latest information from applied biology and medicine, which it feels supports the Church's perennial teaching. But it does not insist that it knows that a complete human person into which God has breathed an immortal soul exists at fertilization, for it adds expressly, "The magisterium [Teaching Office of the Church] has not expressly committed itself to an affirmation of a philosophical nature, but it constantly reaffirms the moral condemnation of any kind of procured abortion. This teaching has not been changed and is unchangeable" (I, 1).

Now, for science. Science answers the question of when human life begins in the same way it answers the question of when animal life begins. When a dog conceives, new canine life begins; when a cow conceives, new bovine life; when a woman conceives, new human life. (Please note that for those who believe that a person comes fully into being only when God infuses an immortal soul, science does not settle the issue of when personhood begins.)

In September, 1970, *California Medicine*, the official journal of the California Medical Association, informed

its readers that the old Judeo-Christian ethic of reverence
for each human life is losing out to society's concern
over population expansion, worry about limited resources, and desire for a higher standard of living.

Since the journal is pro-choice, the following statement which it made cannot be passed off as pro-life
propaganda: "Since the old ethic has not yet been fully
displaced it has been necessary to separate the idea of
abortion from the idea of killing, which continues to be
socially abhorrent. The result has been a curious avoidance of the scientific fact, which everyone really knows,
that human life begins at conception and is continuous
whether intra-or-extra-uterine until death."

The editorial goes on to speak of the "considerable
semantic gymnastics" being used to pretend that abortion does not take human life. It says these gymnastics
would be "ludicrous" but for the fact that they're put
forth "under socially impeccable auspices."[22]

In *The Right To Live; The Right Die*, C. Everett Koop,
former Surgeon General of the United States and prominent surgeon and pediatrician, provides an example of
these "semantic gymnastics" in high places. In 1965, the
American College of Obstetricians and Gynecologists
*changed the definition of human pregnancy*. Until then, everyone accepted that human pregnancy occurred at fertilization. Suddenly, the College *decided that pregnancy
didn't occur until implantation*!

The reality hadn't changed. The new life continued
to be conceived at fertilization.

Hear Dr. Koop: "The term 'post-conceptive contraception' (double-talk of the highest magnitude) and
'post-conceptive fertility control' came into being as syn-
onymous for abortion" (p. 34).

Look closer at this terminology: *contraception* is deliberate prevention of conception; therefore *post-concep-*

*tive* contraception is deliberate prevention of conception *after* conception has occurred!

Whatever the American College of Obstetrics and Gynecology had in mind in changing the definition of conception to refer to a period later than the origin of new human life, it is a change dangerous to that life. It cannot be accepted without the most convincing of reasons. Neither the medical authorities just quoted against the new definition, nor this author, has seen anything approaching such convincing reasons.

In 1982, Congressman Albert Lee Smith of Alabama proposed an amendment to the Federal Insecticide, Fungicide and Rodenticide Bill to address the fact that unborn children are particularly vulnerable to pesticides. The amendment affirmed that human life begins at conception, and required the Environmental Protection Agency to take this into account in its decisions on pesticides. The bill passed, and Congressman George Brown of California, an abortion-on-demand advocate, commended the amendment.[23]

## 14. Even if the new life is human, is it a person at once?

Despite its possession of revelation, and its wisdom gathered over the ages, even the Catholic Church does not claim to answer this question definitively. Therefore, prudence and moral responsibility require us to break the question into two questions, the first theoretical and the second practical: Is the new life a person at once? Must it be treated as a person at once?

The theoretical question is generally asked by those who believe that the human soul is spiritual and therefore comes directly from God by an action of creation. But when? At conception? God has not revealed the moment. But as mentioned in the last question, the Church's document, *Donum Vitae*, says that the latest medical evidence lends further support to the reasons why the Catholic Church teaches that at the first moment of new life, that life must be treated as a person.

That latest medical evidence is primarily the discovery of the genes and chromosome of the genetic code, present in a one-celled new human life at fertilization, the moment of conception. Science states that, from the scientific vantage point, all that is needed to grow into a mature human being is present when fertilization has taken place.

Science can never tell us about souls; it can only tell us that human life has begun. Morality and religion must enter here, and affirm the parents' responsibility to care for that life, since they brought it into being. They also affirm that society must do what is necessary to promote "life, liberty and the pursuit of happiness."

New evidence and new controversies will always appear. Certain medical scientists say that more recent scientific developments amend the scientific position: The zygote or fertilized ovum still needs not only support but additional genetic material from the mother to complete its development. Before its implantation in the uterus is completed some two weeks later, it may even divide and become twins, or deteriorate so that it is no longer human.[24]

But Dr. Jerome Lejeune, considered the father of modern genetics, disagrees. In 1991, long after these claims were made, he testified in a New Jersey case in which Alex Loce and others stormed an abortion clinic to prevent Loce's former fiancee from aborting their child. Lejeune argued that not only do the medical and genetic advances prove that life begins at conception, but that "the human constitution is entirely spelled out," and a "new human being begins its career." The very first cell which results from conception "is a member of the human species." The judge found the evidence conclusive that the eight-week old fetus "was a living person, a human being." But he found Loce guilty because the law of the land permits "legal executions" of the unborn.[25]

Lejeune gave more exhaustive evidence to a Senate Judiciary Committee. Only a couple of key points can be presented here: He said "everybody was agreeing that 'test-tube babies', if produced, would demonstrate the autonomy of the conceptus, over which the test tube has no title of property. Test-tube babies now do exist."

These conflicting scientific claims and opinions only underscore the Church's wisdom, which does not rely on such data for what is a far more fundamental matter: Human beings have cooperated to begin new human life. From then on they have a grave obligation to sustain the human life they have begun. And this teaching, said Pope Paul VI, "has not changed and is unchangeable."[26]

## 15. If the new human life is not a person at once, doesn't that lessen any responsibility toward the new life?

No one can show that a new human life is not a person at once. The best biological and philosophical evidence support the conclusion that it is a person at once. In his personal statements, Pope John Paul II appears to have taken a more definitive stand than in the formal documents of the Church. To pro-life leaders in 1991, Pope John Paul II said: "From conception every human being is a person."[27]

In a secular culture, we must offer a reasoned response from a secular vantage point. From a scientific secular point of view, which neither knows nor accepts anything about souls, new life is human from its first stage of development. Science confirms what people have said for ages, that life begins at conception. Even before modern science developed, Western legal traditions recognized a pre-born child as a person with the right of inheriting estates.

Now we consider the issue from the vantage point of faith. The Catholic faith teaches that God creates and infuses an immortal human soul into the new human life, and thus makes it a person. God has not revealed the instant this takes place, but has placed human life in our care. The fact that God leaves us uninformed about the moment he plays his role surely does not gainsay our responsibility toward the new life. A new human life has begun, called to share the human lot, and, finally, to share eternal life with God. That makes human life sacred in all its stages. Once human beings have cooperated to begin a new human life, they have the grave responsibility to care for it.

We can gain a perspective on Catholic teaching by considering sexuality, conception, and respect for all human life as a continuum. Sexuality is the source of human life, and sexual sins are objectively grave sins. When new human life is originated, it is clear that it is *human* life, and so to kill it is a grave sin, even if we cannot prove beyond the shadow of a doubt that it is already a human person. Someone may argue that to kill one who is certainly a person is a graver sin. Even if that be true, any one of these sins is grave enough to lead to eternal condemnation before God, and must be avoided to inherit eternal life. The Church teaches that no circumstances can justify any of these sinful acts.

The Congregation for the Doctrine of the Faith affirms the gravity of abortion, whatever the biological facts. In its *Declaration on Procured Abortion* it "leaves aside the question of the moment when the soul is infused. There is not a unanimous tradition on this point and authors are as yet in disagreement. . . . It is a philosophical problem from which our moral affirmation remains independent for two reasons: (1) supposing a belated animation, there is still nothing less than a human life, preparing for and calling for a soul in which the nature received from the parents is completed; (2) on the other hand it suffices that this presence of the soul be probable (and one can never prove the contrary) in order that the taking of life involve accepting the risk of killing a man not only waiting for but in possession of his soul." (See footnote 19.)

The American Catholic Hierarchy states: "A human person, nothing more and nothing less, is always at issue once conception has taken place. We expressly repudiate any contradictory suggestion as contrary to Judaeo-Christian traditions inspired by love for life, and Anglo-Saxon legal traditions protective of life and the person" (*Human Life In Our Day*, pp. 27-28).

Many Americans agree with this position. In a 1989 poll, 48% agreed with the statement, "Abortion is the same thing as murdering a child," while only 40% denied that proposition. This seems hopeful, until one learns that a third of those who called abortion murder agreed that "it is sometimes the best course."[28]

Some authors propose arguments which they think support a need to redefine conception. They theorize that the first life conceived is not human, and true conception is later than fertilization by two or more weeks. (For one such author, see the answer to the next question.) The evidence cited from experts throughout these responses is presented as more than weighty enough to show that such a redefinition is not admissible on logical or biological grounds. No solid evidence exists to abandon the prevailing judgment that conception, that is, new human life, begins when a sperm fecundates an egg to form a zygote, the first stage of a human embryo.

Others point out the frequent cases of "wastage," in which biological failures cause a very early miscarriage. From this, they want to draw some inference that new life in its earliest stages is of less consequence. Logic requires the opposite conclusion: that if life is so precarious, the life that survives is even more precious, and requires even greater care.

In summary: We cannot prove that at the moment of conception the new life is already a complete human person. What we can affirm is as follows: (1) The beginning of true human life (not something less) is present at conception; (2) A human person is most likely already present at conception; (3) If, improbably, it is not, it is *destined to become a human person*. Therefore, in abortion, a human person is always at issue; (4) The rights to be protected are not solely those of the new life and its destiny for time and for eternity, but also those of God the Creator, both parents, the nation, and the human race. We all have a stake in the protection of human life.

Respect for human life does not depend on settling the question of when God infuses a soul into a new human being. Biological science affirms what the ancients knew, that human life begins at conception.

Is abortion murder, then? In late abortions, it clearly is. In all cases, it may be murder. Tertullian put it most strongly in early Christianity, when he said 1,700 years ago, "To prevent birth is anticipated murder; it makes little difference whether one destroys a life already born, or does away with it in its nascent stage."[29]

## 16. Would you add any further helpful information on this question of the humanity and personhood of the new human life in the mother?

Since science deals with matter and energy, the biological facts are the only evidence a secular materialist can admit. Pro-choice persons, if they are consistent with the biological facts, have to admit that abortion is the taking of a human life. That life is either already a person or will soon become one. Abortion then is inescapably the taking of human life. Pro-choice people can justify their position, even in part, only if they claim that the new human life is not yet developed enough to enjoy the rights of a person. But who decides that? An individual? A set of Supreme Court Justices? Or the wisdom of the human race informed by the latest evidence?

Consider the wisdom of The Declaration of Independence, which says: "We hold these truths to be self-evident, that all men are created equal." By "self-evident truths" they are referring to the *natural law*.

Forget for a moment the objective rights of the life in the womb, and consider the sense of obligation engraved in the human heart. Can those who brought that life into being, whether believers or unbelievers, feel at peace if they destroy what is clearly human life? The natural law is embedded in people's hearts. To ignore it can lead to psychological agony, and even suicide. These objective realities demand serious consideration in any abortion decision.

Now let us consider a religious person who admits the strong evidence in favor of the conclusion that a human being is a person at conception. Suppose he says, "Yes, but I don't think the soul is infused by God for at least forty days, so I don't have to treat that new life with the responsibility I ought to show a person." Isn't he using his faith to destroy his faithfulness if he uses his uncertainty about the moment a human soul is created as a justification for abortion?

God did not reveal the specifics of his part—only that he breathes into human beings a living soul. So even the wisest of believers did not and do not know when God infuses the soul. As philosophers, they attempted to reason to an answer, but never came to an agreed conclusion. Yet the Fathers of the Church and the great theologians who admitted to this lack of knowledge never dreamed of using it as a reason to permit abortion. They were trying to probe a mystery, not provide a justification for abortion.

St. Augustine inclined to think that the soul was created at conception. St. Thomas Aquinas thought it was later. St. Thomas based his position on the biology of Aristotle, which was over a thousand years old, and completely inaccurate. It knew nothing about the ovum in the woman, or about the nature of the sperm in the man. It taught that the semen of the man used the menstrual blood of the woman to form a new human life, and that neither the semen or the menstrual blood was living. St. Thomas thought that it took 40 days for a male and 90 for a female to prepare a human body for ensoulment.[30] Today we know that both the male and female fetus' heart is beating before a month is out, and that electric brain waves have been detected as early as the 43rd day.

The development of this brain has been under guidance for many days before that by an *entelechy*, a profound guiding energy or soul or principle of life that directs the maturing of a specifically human organ of thought. Can that principle of life be anything less than a rational human soul infused by God? To this writer, it seems impossible. No effect can be greater than its cause. What cause other than a rational soul can prepare for itself a human brain, with centers of judgement and reason and moral decisions, useful only to a rational, spiritual being—a person?

Surely St. Thomas would have changed his theory had he known the biological information about the genetic pattern contained in the living egg and the living sperm, as known today. One cannot claim to know what St. Thomas' new theory would be. But we can say, as many philosophers have, that there no longer seems to be a basis for the Aristotelian theory of delayed animation.

Some still deny the personhood of the embryo in its earliest stages, on one or other grounds: biological, philosophical, theological, social, political. Moralist Germain Grisez gives an overview and rebuttal of their positions in an article entitled, "When do people begin?"[31]

Grisez states: "what is necessary and sufficient to be a human being is to be a whole, bodily individual with a human nature. On this notion, if a human activated ovum has in itself the epigenetic primordia of a human body normal enough to be the organic basis of some intellectual act, that activated ovum is a person. But some activated ova are too abnormal to be people, and some people, including some or all of identical twins, never were activated ova. Thus, most human persons begin at fertilization, although some begin during the next two or three weeks by others' dividing and perhaps also by others' combining" (p. 40).

Thus Grisez thinks that "most human beings begin at fertilization and that both morality and law should consider all of them as persons." He supports his position, on the biological level, with a quote from a recent book which states what most biologists hold: "Fertilization in mammals normally represents the beginning of new life for an individual."[32]

He concludes: "There is a very strong factual and theoretical ground for thinking that almost all of us once

were zygotes. The counterpositions are weak. To be willing to kill what for all one knows is a person is to be
willing to kill a person" (p. 41). And so even those not
convinced that practical doubt is excluded should, in
their moral judgments, treat the earliest embryo as a
person.

Authoritative early Christian writings confirm this
position of Grisez. They show that ignorance of the moment of the soul's infusion in no way justifies abortion.
The first century *Didache* (2:2; 5:2) and the *Letter of
Barnabas* (19:5), basic instructions for early Christians,
declare: "Do not take the life of the fetus by abortion: it is
the work of God." Tertullian, a Father of the Church, and
a lawyer of renown, wrote over 1,700 years ago: "To
prevent birth is anticipated murder; it makes little difference whether one destroys a life already born or does
away with it in its nascent stage. The one who will be a
man is already one."[33]

Fr. Thomas O'Donnell declares: "From the Council
of Elvira (circa A.D. 300) to Vatican II the Catholic
Church has always condemned abortion of the human
fetus as the murder of the innocent." O'Donnell adds
that abortion was sometimes "referred to as 'conditional'
or 'interpretative' homicide."[34] Some scholars don't
agree that abortion has always been considered murder,
but agree it has been condemned as immoral.

Vatican II taught: "God, the Lord of life, has con-
ferred on men the surpassing ministry of safeguarding
life . . . . Therefore, from the moment of conception life
must be guarded with the greatest care, while abortion
and infanticide are unspeakable crimes."[35]

The celebrated Protestant Pastor, Dietrich Bonhoeffer, whose faithfulness to Christ cost him his life
under the Nazis, says somewhere of abortion: "The
simple fact is that God certainly intended to create a

human being and that this nascent human being has been deliberately deprived of his life. And that is nothing but murder." Bonhoeffer and others like Mother Teresa of Calcutta who call abortion murder[36] are speaking from a profound human and faith perspective. Knowing that both human beings and God have set everything in motion to bring a new person into existence, they believe that to willfully destroy that new human life is either murder or tantamount to murder, since it destroys a life to which personhood has been given or promised.

Late abortions clinch the point that our present abortion law legalizes murder. *Roe v. Wade* permits abortions until childbirth, unless states forbid it after viability (before viability, states are not allowed to forbid it).[37] Who can mount any sane claim that these children are not persons? Some of them are born prematurely and survive. Others are legally aborted, and survive even the torment of saline abortions. Still others who are legally aborted very late die as intended. This is murder in any rational analysis.

In at least one case, a doctor was indicted for killing a child which was perfectly viable, but then acquitted because he had reached into the body of the mother and killed the child while it was still in her body. If he had done the same after it had emerged, it would have been manslaughter.[38]

From the perspective of faith, think of what this means for the victim. Our Lord said: "Truly, truly, I say to you, unless one is born of water and the Spirit, he cannot enter the kingdom of God. That which is born of the flesh is flesh, and that which is born of the Spirit is spirit" (Jn 3:5-6). The fate of the eternal life of the unborn child is even more crucial than that of his or her mortal life. This issue will be taken up more fully in question 21.

In summary: Science and faith, each in its own way, have a view of the nature of life in the womb. From both perspectives, abortion is the termination of a new human life whose possession of personhood is supported by strong evidence and philosophical reasoning.

**17. Pro-choice people demand to know why the morality of pro-life people should be imposed on them. What's a sound response?**

This question has already been answered in many ways, but now we answer it head on. It sounds like a fair question, but it is a subjective question. The objective question is: Should the rule of authentic law be imposed on people who want the right to kill unborn innocents? Let us answer that latter question, and then return to the question of "imposing morality."

For the common good, and especially the good of the defenseless, a society must govern itself by just laws. Example: A thief, a rapist, and a murderer might say, "We have chosen an alternate life style," and add, "Why should you impose your morality on us? You can't legislate morality!"

By the sane and common judgment of most people, theirs is not an alternate life style. They lawlessly prey on other human beings. Similarly, to kill the defenseless occupant of the womb is to lawlessly prey on the innocent. Civilization cannot tolerate this.

When people told Reverend Martin Luther King Jr. that morality can't be legislated, he would say that the law could not force people to love their neighbors, but it could curb a lynch mob.

Those who object that "you can't legislate morality" don't seem to understand law. Law either legislates on the basis of morality or it is bad law. Of course, law does not carve out a whole system of morality; it restrains immoral conduct which destroys the common good.

In trying to prove that morality can't be legislated, people cite the failure of the Eighteenth Amendment against intoxicating beverages. But that was bad law because drinking moderately is not immoral. That amendment was like legislating against intercourse instead of fornication or adultery, which are abuses of intercourse.

Now we answer the question *why should pro-life people impose their morality on pro-choice people?* The answer is that they don't. Pro-life people impose neither laws nor morality—and we need to be alert to the difference.

First, we impose no laws. We work through the normal channels of our society for the passage of fair laws to guard unborn children. We employ the normal channels available to everyone in a free society. We make no progress unless voters and legislators and judges take up the cause as they take up other causes. The racial laws were changed, not by a small group imposing their morality, but by a small group who clamored for the country to regain its moral sense—and they succeeded. We do likewise.

Actually, a case was made in *Roe v. Wade* by dissenting Justice Rehnquist that it was the Court which was illegally imposing law on the nation: "The decision here to break the term of pregnancy into three distinct terms and to outline the permissible restrictions the state may impose in each one, for example, partakes more of judicial legislation than it does of a determination of the drafters of the Fourteenth Amendment.

"The fact that a majority of the States, reflecting after all the majority sentiment in those States, have had restrictions on abortion for at least a century seems to me as strong an indication there is that the asserted right to abortion is not 'so rooted in the traditions and conscience of our people as to be ranked as fundamental.'

"To reach its result the Court necessarily has had to find within the scope of the Fourteenth Amendment a right that was apparently completely unknown to the drafters of the amendment. As early as 1821, the first state law dealing directly with abortion was enacted by the Connecticut legislature."[39]

It would be hard to say more clearly, in legal terms, that the Justices who affirmed the decision were illegally legislating. That is, they imposed law on the American people, despite the fact that only the Congress and the President have the right to legislate for the nation. Many other legal minds have since confirmed Rehnquist's judgment, as indicated elsewhere in these answers.

In another abortion decision on the same day (*Doe v. Bolton*), dissenting Justice White, joined by Justice Rehnquist, states even more plainly that the Court has exceeded its authority: "With all due respect, I dissent. I find nothing in the language or history of the Constitution to support the Court's judgment. The court simply fashions and announces a new constitutional right for pregnant mothers and, with scarcely any reason or authority for its action, invests that right with sufficient substance to override most existing state abortion laws."[40]

In the *Thornburg Case*, Justice White stated that decisions which ignore constitutional principles "usurp the people's authority," and such decisions "represent choices that the people have never made and they cannot disavow through corrective legislation." White goes on to argue that for this reason the Court should overrule its 1973 decision legalizing abortion. Chief Justice Burger also stated that the Court should overturn *Roe v. Wade*.

We impose no morality, but to blame anyone for promoting laws based on morality lacks good sense. What else can a good law be based on? Laws against theft, murder, rape and speeding are laws to protect life. Laws to tax people for the operation of government are laws to support life by promoting the life, liberty, and pursuit of happiness of citizens.

The *New York Times*, certainly a liberal paper, admitted in an editorial: "Government must often legislate and enforce morality. . ." (7/31/86). That is only a way of saying we need laws, which are for the lawbreakers.

Strictly speaking, law does not impose morality, but only regulates behavior. Morality is a doctrine or system which specifies right and wrong conduct. Personal morality concerns a person's inner convictions and commitment to right human conduct. In that sense it cannot be imposed, except perhaps by brainwashing.

When we are accused of imposing morality, it seems to be by people who imagine that morality is a subjective concoction of each person or collection of persons who agree about it.

The truth is that right and wrong human conduct is properly based, not on subjectivity, but on reality. The *ius gentium* refers to the laws which the family of nations hold in common. Diverse nations have upheld many of the same laws, such as injunctions against murder. This is possible due to conscience, that inborn sense of right and wrong based on reason and experience. Without such laws, society cannot endure. A most fundamental natural law is the right to life. "The state," wrote Aristotle, "comes into existence that man may live."

Over 2,000 years ago, the Roman statesman Cicero eloquently laid the case for *natural law*:

"True law is right reason in accord with nature. Changeless and everlasting, it imbues all men. By its commands it summons to duty, by its prohibitions, it averts from wrongdoing . . . . To alter the law, or to repeal any part of it, is forbidden by all that is holy, while to abolish it is impossible. We can be freed from it neither by the senate nor by the people, nor need we look outside ourselves for its expounder or interpreter. Nor will there be one law in Rome and another at Athens, one now and another in ages to come. Rather a single sempiternal and immutable law will hold among all nations for all time."[41]

Until the recent public anxiety over "runaway population," the *ius gentium of modern times* defended the unborn. The United Nations' 1959 *Declaration of Human Rights* did so, as we mentioned in an earlier answer.

Laws don't demand a change of inner convictions, but they do demand a certain conduct, an acceptable way of relating to other citizens. Laws require that we all obey, not that we all agree.

So in a free society, laws emerge from the convictions and moral sense of a people. They secure justice, especially for the weak who cannot defend themselves. They impose minimal standards of justice which society needs to flourish and even to exist.

Pro-life people try to restore that moral sense which prevailed before *Roe v. Wade* corrupted it: that abortion is an evil. An old rabbinic proverb says that when you do an evil for the first time, it's horrible to you. If you get used to doing it, you will defy any challenger with the taunt: "What's wrong!" This erosion has affected many Americans since *Roe v. Wade*. We must reverse it.

To draw people to a healthful and reasonable rule of law by the legitimate means available within a society, then, is not to impose morality. It is a service to the common good.

Pro-life people can do no less than appeal to all citizens to defend each innocent unborn life because of its sacredness; and to use their political rights to work for a rule of law that will guarantee that unborn babies enjoy full protection of their right to life. We can and should do this by appealing to the moral and religious sense of the whole people. We don't attempt to force our own religious faith on anyone. But we are aware that many of our religious convictions do not depend on faith alone. The civil rights movement furnishes an example: A lively Christian or Jewish faith impelled many to take up the cause, but non-believers too could support it as a sheer human issue.

What issue is more human than respect and reverence for life in the womb, which is the only future of humanity?

## 18. What is your opinion of pro-life people who think they should not try to influence the position of pro-choice people?

Whatever their good intentions, they leave the unborn with no real defense. It is not enough to be privately opposed to abortion. A person whose conscience does not urge action in the public forum should earnestly examine that conscience to decide what to do. A human being is a social being, and a true conscience is a social conscience. Most of us could say what Jesus said: "He who is not with me is against me, and he who does not gather with me scatters" (Matt 12:30). Burning human issues demand commitment, not neutrality.

An especially deplorable example of this irresponsible neutrality is the politician or legislator who states: "I'm personally opposed to abortion, but I think people should be allowed to choose." We elect officials to draft responsible public policies, not to drift with the tide. Some of these self-professed straddlers even support public funding for legal abortions. They are in fact pro-abortion in their public policy.

Isn't it clear? Anyone who does not oppose the pro-choice camp fails in the duty to oppose the killing of the unborn. Supporting pro-choice policies is to support the killing of the unborn. How can that be called pro-life? If you look at their actions, you can't tell one from the other. Morality is about human actions, whether in thought, word, or deed.

Voters who call themselves pro-life but vote for known pro-choice candidates need to examine this issue urgently. They may say that the pro-life issue is only one issue, but it is the issue of our times. It is the issue concerning the value of our lives and all human lives: Is life inviolable or not? Admittedly, there are times when no viable candidate for a particular office is pro-life. In such cases we pray and reflect to make the best decision possible, keeping our priorities straight.

In any case to be pro-life and yet refuse to be socially active against the evil of abortion is clearly immoral. Once again I quote the Book of Leviticus: "Nor shall you stand by idly when your neighbor's life is at stake" (19:16).*

## 19. Shouldn't the Church reverse its stand against contraception and sterilization and allow birth control as a solution to the abortion problem?

The answer has to be *No*. Volumes are needed to give all the reasons. Four main reasons will be cited here, and each will be explained briefly: (1) The end does not justify the means, and contraception is an evil means; (2) Contraception leads not to a decrease but to an increase in abortions; (3) Contraceptives themselves cause the greatest number of abortions; (4) A highly reliable form of birth control called Natural Family Planning is now available. It uses no drugs, chemicals or devices. It is completely natural and moral. We now have a practical, moral solution to the problem of family planning.

First, the end does not justify the means, and contraception is an evil means. Already in the Old Testament, Onan practiced contraception and God punished him: "But Onan knew that the offspring would not be his; so when he went in to his brother's wife he spilled the semen on the ground, lest he should give offspring to his brother. And what he did was displeasing in the sight of the LORD, and he slew him also" (Gen 38:9-10).

Pope Paul VI condemned the evil of contraception in his great Encyclical, *Humanae Vitae* ("On the Regulation of Birth"). Contraceptives, led by the pill, continue to sweep the world. They leave a swath of moral, physical, psychological and social destruction, much of which the Pope prophetically predicted.

The pill injures the health of women, and statistics show it can bring premature death. The major IUDs have been pulled from the U.S. market because of their health risk and the resulting fear of lawsuits. Sterilization (a method of birth control that cannot reliably be reversed), has failings similar to other contraceptives. It makes the human body less than it should be, shuns the loving drama of total mutual self-giving with all its consequences, and invites extramarital liaisons.

Contraceptives are immoral because they violate the natural law by separating what nature and nature's God have joined together in marital intercourse: lovemaking and openness to new life. Hasn't intercourse often been called the procreative act?

Until 1930, all Christian Churches condemned contraception as a violation of God's law. The Catholic Church and certain other churches and religions still do so.

The American bishops, in their 1968 letter, *Human Life in Our Day*, treat this matter. They recognize: "Married couples faced with conflicting duties are often caught in agonizing crises of conscience" such as the one of wanting to express their love in the marital act, yet not wanting more children. But the bishops support Paul VI in reminding all that "no one following the teaching of the Church can deny the objective evil of artificial contraception itself."

Pope John Paul II, in his global travels, has warned the world against contraception. In his Apostolic Exhortation, *The Role of the Christian Family in the Modern World*, he teaches, in accord with Vatican II, that the conjugal act, because of the nature of the human person, must "preserve the full sense of mutual self-giving and human procreation in the context of true love." Then he describes the personal harm done by contraception: "When couples, by means of recourse to contraception, separate these two meanings that God the Creator has inscribed in the being of man and woman and in the dynamism of their sexual communion, they act as 'arbiters' of the divine plan, and they 'manipulate' and degrade human sexuality—and with it themselves and their married partner—by altering its value of total self-giving" (n. 32).

Second, contraception, in practice, has led to increased numbers of abortions. The world-wide opponent of contraception and abortion, and promoter of Natural Family Planning, sociologist Fr. Paul Marx, OSB, gives untiring witness to the fact that wherever contraception creeps in, abortions escalate.

The contraception-abortion connection is easy to trace. Contraception separates sex from morals, intercourse from reproduction, and sexual activity from responsibility. Teenagers become increasingly sexually active. Sexual promiscuity spreads to all classes and ages. Sexual activism naturally produces an increase in pregnancies. Teenagers especially do not use contraceptives reliably, and no contraceptive is fully reliable (according to an article in *Family Planning Perspectives* for Sept./Oct., 1980, 30% of out-of-wedlock pregnancies among teens occurred while contraceptives were being used).

A recent article headlined: "More Girls Are Sexually Active, Study Shows." Fewer than a third of 15- to 17-year-old girls were active in 1982, as against nearly 40% in 1990. The article says the pregnancy rate went down because contraceptives were more in use; but while the *rate* went down, the *number* of pregnancies went up, because of the increase in the number of active girls.[42] Only God knows how many undetected conceptions and abortions resulted from the abortifacient effect of the contraceptives.

When, early in this century, Margaret Sanger began the contraceptive movement headed today by Planned Parenthood, her war cry was that contraception is better than abortion. Today, Planned Parenthood is the leading proponent of abortion.

In *Family Planning Perspectives* (Jan., 1971), Philip Cutright called for universal sex ed in the schools, nationwide birth control clinics, and legalized backup abortion. Cutright admitted that sex ed and contraception would not solve the abortion problem. He even admitted that in areas where contraceptives were provided to teenagers, pregnancies skyrocketed.

Then why did he pursue his program? To break down the "pseudo-moral barriers" in the public mind. As he explains it, the real problem is neither premarital sexual activity nor premarital pregnancy. What *is* the problem, then? Let Cutright explain: "The supposed ill effects of premarital sex have never been documented, so long as premarital sex did not lead to an illicit pregnancy that was carried to term. It is the control of these unwanted pregnancies—not the control of premarital sex—that is the problem." In other words, abortion is not a problem but a solution, if only it were not "controlled."

Does Cutright's "solution" work? In 1970, 300,000 out-of-wedlock teens got pregnant. About two-thirds of these girls and women gave birth, and some one-third had abortions. Then, in 1973, the Supreme Court legalized abortion, as Cutright and the other pro-choicers advocated. In addition, the government began to fund birth control clinics.

The result: By 1980, almost half a million unwed teenagers had abortions, and more than 250,000 gave birth. In other words, the teenage abortion rate had gone up five-fold. In addition, the number of teenage out-of-wedlock deliveries had *increased* by a third. Cutright's solution had solved nothing! It had increased both abortions and out-of-wedlock births![43]

How far are extremists willing to carry such "solutions"? In 1981, *The Church of England's Children's Society* published a booklet, "Family Planning for Young People under Sixteen." Under sixteen! English law forbids intercourse with a girl under sixteen! But that did not stop the "Society" from publishing its "position paper."

Is contraception indeed the way to prevent abortion? Or a way to add to the number of victims?

Thirdly, contraceptives themselves cause the greatest number of abortions. The Good Friday, 1985 issue of *Catholics United For Life* entitled: "Surgical Abortion Has Become A Minor Problem" highlighted the dilemma. The article states that while some 5,000 surgical abortions are performed each day in the U.S.: "there are, at the very least, five times that number of babies being murdered by the pill or the IUD." The article presents a chart of various birth control pills and IUDs, and explains how they work, as noted in *The Physician's Desk Reference*. As the chart reports, they often prevent the newly-conceived baby from achieving implantation (nidation) in its mother's womb. The new human life is starved to death in seven to nine days.

In *Birth Control And The Marriage Covenant* (p. 15), John Kippley also discusses abortions produced by contraceptives. His conclusion: "In short, the death toll from the IUD and the Pill exceeds that of the Nazi Holocaust—each year—in the United States alone." He estimates a worldwide figure of 150 million non-surgical abortions via the IUD alone.

In 1991, the Holy See's Pontifical Council for the Laity issued a document, "In the Service of Life." Commenting on recent medical developments, it reports on the: "increasingly closer connection which has developed between contraception and abortion.

Today, as well as devices (such as the IUD), chemical compounds are under experimentation and in use which are at the same time contraceptive and abortifacient, or which have been manufactured and put into research as abortifacients pure and simple.

Until now, the connection between contraception and abortion has been mainly psychological and sociological, whereas today the connection has become biological and functional in nature. At times women and, in the case of some compounds, even doctors are unaware of this" (Part I).

This means that many people involved in pro-life marches have been practicing abortion unwittingly themselves through their contraceptives.

Can anyone in possession of these facts judge that contraception is a way out of the abortion holocaust?

Fourthly, the marvelous news is that a completely moral and highly reliable form of birth control called Natural Family Planning (NFP) is now available. NFP is the God-given solution to the abortion problem. Unless we all lend a hand to make it known, the holocaust will continue indefinitely and grow to numbers that stun the soul. Isn't it possible that couples who use abortifacient contraceptives have conceived dozens of children of whom they are not even aware?

## 20. Would you say more about natural family planning as a way out of the abortion holocaust?

Natural Family Planning (NFP) is a couple controlled form of family planning. It works through fertility awareness combined with coordinated abstinence. It is a shared method that is moral, safe, and effective.

It works through the wonder of fertility awareness. Since the days of the now obsolete calendar rhythm method, medical research has developed two methods of fertility awareness: The Basal Body Temperature Method (BBT), and the Ovulation Method (OM). Both are based on the following medical fact: During the whole of each cycle, a woman can conceive only within a period of about 12-to-24 hours after an ovum (egg) has been released by ovulation and before it disintegrates.

NFP does not manipulate the body with chemicals or interfere with the act of union in any way. Instead, the couple uses their fertility awareness to harmonize their love-making with their family planning objectives.

The Basal Body Temperature Method is founded on the scientific fact that, shortly after ovulation, a woman's body temperature rises. By reading her temperature daily, a woman can learn when she has passed into the infertile post-ovulation phase. During the infertile phase, the likelihood of conception is almost nil.

The Ovulation Method is based on this fact: following menstruation, most women experience a dry vaginal sensation followed by the advent of sticky mucus, and finally by a wet sensation marked by wet, slippery egg-white-like mucus. The latter mucus alerts the couple: Ovulation is about to occur. She is fertile! Intercourse now is likely to produce a child.

To avoid conception, the couple abstains, usually from six to twelve days, until the decline/disappearance of mucus signals that the non-fertile post-ovulation phase has begun.

The BBT and the OM are frequently combined in practice, to produce a double-check method called the Sympto-Thermal Method. Since the "calendar" in NFP is the woman's own body, which she "reads" in each unique cycle, the method works even for women with irregular cycles, even during post-partum and pre-menopause.

The stories of the discovery of NFP are fascinating, and the experience of NFP is a true adventure as well as a godsend to many appreciative couples. One of the tragedies of our time is that this gift of God has not been appreciated for what it is—a far more important development than the control of atomic energy—for it is the human, moral, rational, and religious control of the greatest energy in the world, human life. (For an overview of NFP see the author's booklet, *Natural Family Planning: Why it succeeds,* Daughters of St. Paul).

NFP should be learned from qualified teachers. NFP courses of two-to-three sessions are likely to be available in your area. For literature or course information, contact your pastor, your Catholic Chancery, or one of the national organizations listed in the attached endnote.[44]


### 21. Who is most guilty in an abortion, the woman who has it, the child's father who pressures her, or the physicians and others who profit by it?

*The Code Of Canon Law* states: "A person who procures a successful abortion incurs an automatic excommunication" (Canon 1398). This applies not only to the woman who has an abortion, but to all accomplices without whose efforts she would not have the abortion (Canon 1329). Since these canons are based on the nature of the moral law, they indicate that the grave responsibility for an abortion can fall on a number of people in each case. However, this penalty falls only on those who act freely, knowingly, willfully, and obstinately, and with knowledge of the penalty.

We have no desire to measure and mete out guilt, but to help all responsible for abortion to realize its gravity. We plead with them to shun it for everyone's good: the persons involved, the children yet unborn, and society itself.

The pregnant girl or woman tempted to abortion is often influenced by the corrupt values of our society. It pressures and seduces women into irresponsible sexual activity, then pushes them to have an abortion at a time when they are in emotional turmoil, especially if young and unwed. In many cases, mother and child are simply the victims of the sins of others.

To do more than wring our hands at these evils, we must focus on the corruption of our society, so we can take action against it.

The abortion polls cited earlier make it clear that Americans do not favor the libertine law on abortion. Judge John T. Noonan points out that the seven justices responsible for our law: "invoke the freedom of women but ignore what American women believe and want." He adds: "The liberty of abortion is acting as its proponents expected it to act: It is reducing the birthrate by increasing the number of abortion deaths."[45] In other words, by legalizing abortion, the population-control idealogues used women as pawns. The Supreme Court justices whose ruling allowed easy access to abortion, and legislators who enact such laws, bear a tremendous responsibility to God and society.

The Catholic League for Religious and Civil Rights has charged: "Planned Parenthood's youth activities amount, in effect, to a positive encouragement of sexual activities among teenagers. Showering young people with contraceptives and provocative literature results in a tremendous peer pressure that makes teenagers who do not engage in sex feel abnormal. Planned Parenthood, like certain unscrupulous businesses, is creating a demand for its own services."

Women who have regretted and grieved over their abortions recount how society often forced them into it. They have founded organizations like WE (Women Exploited) and WEBA (Women Exploited By Abortion). They inform and support other women on the verge of falling into the same trap.

They tell of parents who pressure their unmarried daughters to abort; of boyfriends or husbands who "don't want to face the responsibility of supporting the baby they helped to create"; and of counselors and medics using evasive talk about "gently removing the contents of the uterus." Too late, these women woke up to the face that "what they were doing was killing my baby." A terrible burden of guilt devastated them.

Women are told: "Abortion is safer than having a tooth pulled." They are not told of the women who die from abortion, or of the many whom abortion renders sterile. For these, the children they consigned to death are fated to be their last. Abortion robs them of motherhood forever.

Goaded by false and alarmist propaganda about the "population explosion," our culture often treats childbearing as an offense against society—though where society would be without childbearing is evident to anyone.[46]

Says one girl driven to abortion: "Why was my first pregnancy treated like a disease, something too horrible to tell anyone about? The injustice of it nearly drove me to suicide."

It does drive some to suicide. Who knows how

many? In 1981, suicide was the third leading cause of death among 15- to 24-year-olds. In that same year an article in the medical journal, *Pediatrics*, alerted doctors to the danger that teenagers who have undergone abortions are potential suicides.

The article even specified the date such girls might attempt self-destruction: the date on which their child would have been born. By 1986, suicide ranked as the second leading cause of death among 15- to 19-year-olds. We know that some of the young women among them were driven to suicide by abortion, but what about men? How many male suicides are rooted in an unendurably bad self-image mushrooming out of the way they dropped the pregnant women in their lives, or drove them to abortion?

Every normal woman, like Eve, identifies herself as actually or potentially "mother of the living." Degrading that valid and honorable self-identification is a grave crime of our society. Girls and boys seldom hear such sound advice as Mother Teresa gave to a Radcliffe graduating class: on the wedding day: "the most beautiful thing is to give a virgin heart, a virgin body, a virgin soul."

All too often girls are not given the view of pregnancy expressed by humorist Erma Bombeck. Asked if, given the chance to live life over, she would change anything, she answered: "Instead of wishing away nine months of pregnancy and complaining about the shadow over my feet, I'd have cherished every minute of it and realized that the wonderment growing inside me was to be my only chance in life to assist God in a miracle."

Hasn't God, who is Love, honored mothers by portraying their love as the nearest to his own? "Can a woman forget her child, that she should have no compassion on the son of her womb? Even these may forget, yet I will not forget you" (Is 49:15).

Woe to a society who makes mothers forget! One

aborted mother, when the tragedy had penetrated to her heart, wrote of *how* our society made her forget: "Student newspapers, radio, television, magazines and freeway advertisements all depicted the glory of abortion."

No mother and father really want to hear their child say to them in their hearts: "You conceived me in your passion, but you wouldn't let me enter into your love."

It is our responsibility to understand the degraded and dehumanized experience of these women who have faced a pregnancy with no support from husband or paramour, parents, friends or society. Our compassion for them as victims will assist them to recover and to help other women ward off the same fate.

But as we sympathize with the victimized mother, we should also recall that other victim, the baby. It is not enough to sing a dirge because the child will never know the beauty of earth, the sight of the stars or the joys of marriage. The more serious reality is that the slaughtered unborn may never know the joys of God. As the respected theologian, Fr. Bertrand de Margerie, SJ, pointed out in an article in *L'Osservatore Romano*, no Church document has changed the traditional teaching Pius XII affirmed, that baptism is the only sure means of salvation for human beings who die before the age of reason.[47]

He urges that the aborted child be baptized if at all possible. Often it is impossible, even if someone present would attempt it. Abortion too often dismembers the child in the womb.

We face another weighty consideration, especially for those who tend to downplay the seriousness of abortion because they hold the theory that the soul is created after the body is more developed in the womb. If, as the theory of delayed animation holds, the soul of the occupant of the womb has not yet been created by the time of a very early abortion, what is the consequence? Does the thought of the person he planned to create remain forever in the mind of God? As in the case of non-baptism, we can hope that God would still create that soul, and raise that body at the parousia, but of such matters we have no knowledge.

Instead of trying to apportion the guilt of others, let's do better. Let's meditate on the guilt we share if we don't do our part to oppose abortion. Let's take up vocal, political and legal arms against the killing of the unborn. Let's scorn any criticism leveled at us for putting the issue before our own concerns and comforts when we vote.

Haven't many of us wondered how good people in Germany remained silent and passive during the Holocaust? *Were* they good? And we don't have the Gestapo to threaten us!

To help distressed women and unborn children is not a favor we bestow; it is a solemn duty we fulfill. "Nor shall you stand by idly when your neighbor's life is at stake. I am the LORD" (Lev 19:16).*

The Holy See's Pontifical Council on the Family, in its document, *In the Service of Life* (Part II), says: "The words of Christ can be applied to the unborn, the most needy and defenseless of human beings: 'Inasmuch as you have done this to the least of my brethren you have done it to Me.'" God forbid that Christ should say to us: "I was endangered in the womb, and you did nothing to save me."

## 22. How can a woman weighed down with the sin of abortion find reconciliation with God and his Church?

Prayer and penance obtain forgiveness of sin. If the woman has heartfelt repentance, angelic tongues are not eloquent enough to express the tender mercy God wants to shower on her. She need only confess her sin to the

Lord who will generously grant pardon. If she is a Catholic, she should also confess to the Church in the Sacrament of Reconciliation.

If remorse burdens her, but she has not yet come to true repentance, she needs to take the steps that will help her find it. She must strengthen her faith in God's willingness to forgive every repented sin; grow in motivation to seek forgiveness by considering the good it will bring; come to realize that, bad and hopeless as she may feel, God can restore her beyond hope, as he has done so many others; trust not in any goodness of her own, but in God's goodness; count on the power of Jesus her crucified Savior to wash away every sin; realize that to ask for forgiveness honors and pleases God; and, when she has asked for and experienced forgiveness, she must fight against guilt feelings that will try to creep back. What follows will trace these stages of repentance.

To read and pray over Scripture will help her believe that God will forgive everything and can repair anything. Like the repentant woman whom Jesus forgives in chapter seven of Luke's Gospel, and chapter eight of John's Gospel, she will move from chronic guilt to forgiveness and peace.

She may be tempted to think God will forgive other sins, but not abortion. But abortion is certainly not the worst sin. The worst sin is hatred of God, whom we should love above all.[48] God forgives even that sin to the repentant.

She should motivate herself by thinking about what forgiveness will mean to her. To be forgiven is to experience the melting tenderness of God's embrace. It is to rise from the ashes of her own self-destruction as God wondrously raises her. It is to learn that God can not only restore her, but lift her to a nobler life than she ever lived before. St. Paul marveled at how God brings good out of evil: "We know that in everything God works for good with those who love him, who are called according to his purpose" (Rom 8:28).

That is why the Church can mourn the terrible sin of Adam, and yet exult in the *Easter Proclamation:* "O happy fault, O necessary sin of Adam, which gained for us so great a Redeemer!"

Thus the Church professes faith in God's word and grows in it. No sin is stronger than the immensity of God's tender love. Both Old and New Testaments agree to that. "Come now, let us reason together, says the LORD: though your sins are like scarlet, they shall be as white as snow; though they are red like crimson, they shall become like wool."

Once on TV in Japan, Mother Teresa assured women of God's readiness to forgive. Until midnight, weeping women phoned in to seek consolation from her.

Scripture will help a woman see that she need trust only in God's goodness. It has been said that *mercy is love's second name*, and that is true of God's love beyond any other: "In this is love, not that we loved God but that he loved us and sent his Son to be the expiation for our sins" (1 Jn 4:10).

She can count on the power of Jesus her crucified Savior to wash away all her sins. At the Last Supper Jesus spoke of that expiation for sin: "And he said to them, 'This is my blood of the covenant, which is poured out for many'" (Mk 14:24). Can she still think that the blood of the God-man can cleanse any sin but hers? The Church cries out in one of her hymns that one drop of his blood could wash away the sins of the world.

Jesus understands her burden of sin. "Come to me, all who labor and are heavy laden, and I will give you rest. Take my yoke upon you, and learn from me; for I am gentle and lowly in heart, and you will find rest for your souls" (Mt 11:28-9). Who is more *burdened* than a woman whose sin has cost her her child?

She needs to gain the wonderful insight into love which will help her see that to ask forgiveness is to honor her Savior-God and atone for her sin. She can recall that the people of God are called the spouse of God. A human example will illustrate this. Doesn't a spouse who is not only unfaithful, but then shows no interest or confidence in being forgiven and reunited, add a second and perhaps more cruel sin? So too the Divine Spouse is wounded at heart if a sinner will not trust in his love and forgiveness. In the touching book of Hosea God himself explains these truths.

Will she not be moved by the discovery that to beg Jesus for forgiveness is not just to request his mercy, but to *show him mercy*? To fail to ask is to waste the blood his love poured out for our redemption. It is to turn her back on her eternal Father who knew her sin beforehand, yet sent his Son to be her Savior at such a cost.

To trust Jesus' mercy is to show mercy to him in his agony in the garden, when he looked through time and space to us all. To contemplate Jesus hanging on the cross for her, and grieve over her sin against him heals the wound of his pierced heart. It is to fulfill the word of the prophet Zechariah: "And I will pour out on the house of David and the inhabitants of Jerusalem a spirit of compassion and supplication, so that, when they look on him whom they have pierced, they shall mourn for him, as one mourns for an only child, and weep bitterly over him, as one weeps over a first-born" (12:10).

Jesus' parable of the prodigal son, which applies equally to the prodigal daughter, brings this out. When the wayward son decides to go home, it is because he sees there is no place else for him—a truth deeper than he realizes. He has no hope to return to what he was. He thinks his self-destruction is irreversible. The best he hopes for is to be a servant in his father's house.

How wrong he is! How he underestimates the

power of his father's love! How great his father's joy! It is the joy of not only having his son back, but of raising him from the death of his despair, and restoring his self-worth: "It was fitting to make merry and be glad, for this your brother was dead, and is alive; he was lost, and is found'" (Lk 15:32).[49] Can anyone doubt that the Father finds this same joy when a woman repents her abortion? He is anxious to put her sin from her "as far as the east is from the west, so far does he remove our transgressions from us" (Ps 103:12).

All of this is hers if she will open herself to it. Jesus announces: "The time is fulfilled, and the kingdom of God is at hand; repent, and believe in the gospel" (Mk 1:15).

Despite all this, she may resist admitting her sin even to herself because she remembers all the pressures and helplessness she felt. But she can be sure that the God-man who said: "Judge not, and you will not be judged; condemn not, and you will not be condemned; forgive, and you will be forgiven" (Lk 6:37), will weigh all she went through better than she can. She needs to confess that abortion is wrong, and for the rest throw herself into God's arms, and tell him she accepts his judgment concerning her share of the fault.

She can be helped by King David's experience as he came to terms with his sin: "When I declared not my sin, my body wasted away through my groaning all day long." At last, guilt and suffering led him to admission and confession: "I acknowledged my sin to thee, and I did not hide my iniquity; I said, 'I will confess my transgressions to the Lord'; then you did forgive the guilt of my sin" (Ps 32:3, 5).

*The instant she confesses her sin to God, and tells of her sorrow, above all for offending him, her eternal Father, her sin is gone.*

After that, she will have to resist further guilt feelings. She must spurn them if they try to creep back. Remember that forgiveness is objective. A grievous sin is a deed which results in a certain state of affairs. The deed is done; it can't be undone. The state of affairs can be set right. It consists in a broken relationship with God. Once she has repented and been forgiven, her relationship with God is healed and restored. To express her trust in God she owes it to both God and herself to discount and reject further guilt feelings.

The Catholic, after an act of perfect contrition such as just described, is forgiven. But the responsibility to receive the Sacrament of Reconciliation before receiving Holy Communion remains. The Lord willed this, for he said to his Apostles: "If you forgive the sins of any, they are forgiven; if you retain the sins of any, they are retained" (Jn 20:23). This too is a special mercy of God. By sacramentally declaring God's forgiveness, the priest by divine authority provides a reassuring human expression of forgiveness that seems almost necessary to feel fully forgiven.

It is so easy to fall back into former states of feeling guilty. Special safeguards may be necessary: find a good spiritual director; appeal to the Blessed Mother daily for her tender help; develop devotion to the Divine Mercy by practices recommended by Blessed Faustina, such as to do deeds of mercy for others, and to recall Christ's redemptive death for her each day at three o'clock.[50]

Her sorrow for sin will remain, but that is love grieving, not guilt. We need to grieve over our sins and to make reparation to the heart of Jesus by deeds well done. If history repeats itself, some of those women who repent of abortion will, like the sinners Mary Magdalene, Augustine, and many others, become saints of the future. "Therefore I tell you, her sins, which are many, are forgiven, for she loved much; but he who is forgiven little, loves little" (Lk 7:47).

These truths of forgiveness apply also to others who have been involved in abortion: spouses, boyfriends, doctors, nurses. Many women and men who have repented of being party to abortion have gone on to do great pro-life service, trying to save many more lives than they ended.

WEBA, Women Exploited By Abortion, have followed that path, and done untold good. So have many others, like Dr. Bernard Nathanson, with his lectures, and his books, *Aborting America*, and *The Abortion Papers*.

To become friends, through an organization like WEBA, with other women who have had an abortion and been reconciled with God is a great help to cling to God's forgiveness. To participate in some service in defense of life as WEBA provides seems almost necessary to thank the Lord for his goodness, and fend off bouts of depression and other wayward emotional states that we sinners are heir to.

"Project Rachel" is a ministry in the Catholic Church which specializes in helping women who have had abortions be reconciled and healed. Their address is: Project Rachel; National Office of Post-Abortion Reconciliation and Healing; St. John's Center; 3680 S. Kinnickinnic Ave.; Milwaukee, WI 53207 (Phone: 414-483-4141).

### 23. What does the Bible teach about abortion?

You won't find the word *abortion* in a book like *Nelson's Complete Concordance of the New American Bible*. The Bible never mentions abortion. That doesn't mean it teaches us nothing about abortion. The Bible doesn't spell out every grave sin, but only those which were common, like murder, theft, and sex between non-married persons.

Though admirable in so many ways, Protestant Evangelist Billy Graham, when asked if he had any teaching on abortion, said he did not, for the Bible doesn't speak of it. His position exposes the inadequacy of biblical fundamentalism. It also manifests the wisdom of Christ in giving us the gifts of tradition and the successors of Peter and the rest of the twelve apostles to be the authoritative interpreters of the Bible.

John Connery examines the Jewish legal tradition on abortion in Old Testament times and the times of Christ. He notes that the Jews did not have the severe penalty for abortion imposed on a woman by their Assyrian neighbors: impalement and denial of burial. But he asserts: "An examination of the Jewish tradition in pre-Christian and early Christian times reveals an attitude which recognizes abortion as wrong."[51]

The Catholic sense of the Bible draws endless lessons from both Old and New Testaments about the evil of abortion, just as it does about many other sins not explicitly mentioned in Scripture.

The new *Catechism of the Catholic Church* lists many sins not enunciated in the Bible, such as failing to vote, drunken driving, forging checks, drug abuse and tax evasion.[52] These modern sins either did not exist in biblical times, or, like drug abuse, were relatively rare. The Church, appointed interpreter of the Bible, condemns them because they offend against the Ten Commandments and/or the law of charity: "Love your neighbor as yourself." For instance, it's clear that Scripture implicitly condemns forging checks when it says: "You shall not steal."

Abortion, however, was known and practiced in biblical times, as the Assyrian prohibition referred to above indicates. From either the writing or the spirit of Hippocrates, "the father of medicine," Greek physician of the fourth century B.C., comes the well-known

Hippocratic Oath. It forswears abortion: "I will give no deadly medicine to anyone if asked—nor suggest any such counsel—and in like manner I will not give to any woman a pessary to produce abortion."[53]

Why, then, does the Bible not condemn abortion explicitly? First, abortion was rare among the Jews. The Bible indicates that they esteemed children. The chosen people cherished and loved children and considered them one of God's great blessings. The Bible often praises the fruitful wife as blessed and honored. Sterility was a catastrophe. "Lo, sons are a heritage from the LORD, the fruit of the womb a reward. Like arrows in the hand of a warrior are the sons of one's youth. Happy is the man who has his quiver full of them! He shall not be put to shame when he speaks with his enemies in the gate" (Ps 127:3-5; and see Ps 128).

To understand the implicit scriptural teaching on abortion, it helps to remember that abortion is a sin against both human life and against marriage.

It is a sin against human life. The Church's *Declaration on Procured Abortion* (n. 5) quotes and comments on pertinent scriptural texts: "'Death was not God's doing, he takes no pleasure in the extinction of the living' (Wis 1:13). . . . On the human level, 'it was the devil's envy that brought death into the world' (Wis 2:24). Introduced by sin, death remains bound up with it: death is the sign and fruit of sin. But there is no final triumph for death. Confirming faith in the Resurrection, the Lord proclaims in the Gospel: 'God is God, not of the dead, but of the living' (Mt 22:32). And death like sin will be definitively defeated by resurrection in Christ (cf. 1 Cor 15:20-27). Thus we understand that human life, even on this earth, is precious. Infused by the Creator, life is again taken back by him (cf. Gen 2:7; Wis 15:11). It remains under his protection: man's blood cries out to him (cf. Gen 4:10) and he will demand an account of it, 'for in the image of God man was made' (Gen 9:5-6). The commandment of God is formal: 'You shall not kill' (Ex 20:13)."

The Book of Exodus has several passages that are meaningful in our present struggle with abortion. Those who think abortion is acceptable because commonly done should ponder the words: "You shall not follow a multitude to do evil; nor shall you bear witness in a suit, turning aside after a multitude, so as to pervert justice" (23:2); and also the passage: "Keep far from a false charge, and do not slay the innocent and righteous, for I will not acquit the wicked" (23:7).

The Book of Wisdom tells us: "But ungodly men by their words and deeds summoned death" (1:16). In the Book of Sirach we read: "Wisdom exalts her sons and gives help to those who seek her. Whoever loves her loves life, and those who seek her early will be filled with joy" (4:11-12). The Book of Deuteronomy declares: "I call heaven and earth to witness against you this day, that I have set before you life and death, blessing and curse; therefore choose life, that you and your descendants may live, loving the LORD your God, obeying his voice, and cleaving to him" (30:19-20). Clearly, respecters and lovers of human life are friends of God, the author of life.

Abortion is a sin against the gifts of sex and marriage. When God created the first man and woman: "And God blessed them, and God said to them, 'Be fruitful and multiply, and fill the earth and subdue it'" (Gen 1:28). After God had created human beings: "God saw everything that he had made, and behold, it was very good" (Gen 1:31). In the light of these passages, is it not evident that it is seriously sinful to destroy the fruit of the womb, the life God found very good?

Psalm 139 reflects with wonder on the very beginnings of human life in the womb: "For you did form my inward parts, you did knit me together in my mother's womb. I praise thee, for you are fearful and wonderful. Wonderful are your works! You know me right well" (Ps 139:13-14). In Jeremiah, God speaks to the prophet: "Before I formed you in the womb I knew you, and before you were born I consecrated you; I appointed you a prophet to the nations" (1:5).

When a biblical woman conceived, she didn't think of what was in her womb as a "product of conception." She affirmed: "I am with child," as Bathsheba said to David of the child they had conceived by adultery (cf. 2 Sam 11:5). Nor did David even consider trying to destroy the child, though the situation caused him serious trouble.

Pagans used to offer their children in sacrifice to their false gods, but the true God would never permit such a horror: "You shall not do so to the LORD your God; for every abominable thing which the LORD hates they have done for their gods; for they even burn their sons and their daughters in the fire to their gods" (Deut 12:31).

Despite this warning, some of the Chosen People fell into human sacrifice as some Christians fall into abortion: "They sacrificed their sons and their daughters to the demons; they poured out innocent blood, the blood of their sons and daughters, whom they sacrificed to the idols of Canaan; and the land was polluted with blood. Thus they became unclean by their acts, and played the harlot in their doings"(Ps 106:37-39).

But in the end, the Chosen People stamped out such wanton crime: "These parents who murder helpless lives, you did will to destroy by the hands of our fathers, that the land most precious of all to thee might receive a worthy colony of the servants of God" (Wis 12:6-7).

God the Father tested Abraham by calling him to

sacrifice Isaac, but did not permit the boy to be sacrificed. He only used Abraham as a figure of himself, for the Father's Son, Jesus, was to be sacrificed. In the case of Jesus, the Father allowed his Son's death as a ransom for our salvation, but he did not cause it. As St. Gregory Nazianzen said, it is unthinkable that the Father wanted the gore of his own Son. How, then, can God not find it an unspeakable sin when fathers and mothers kill their own children by abortion as a kind of sacrifice to their own ends?

The child is not the property of father or mother, but of God, as the mother of the seven sons martyred for their faith knew so well: "I do not know how you came into being in my womb. It was not I who gave you life and breath, nor I who set in order the elements within each of you. Therefore the Creator of the world, who shaped the beginning of man and devised the origin of all things, will in his mercy give life and breath back to you again, since you now forget yourselves for the sake of his laws" (2 Macc 7:22-23).

At least some of the chosen people, possessors of the Hebrew Scriptures, saw abortion as a grievous matter. Writing about 1,900 years ago, Josephus said: "the law has commanded to raise all children and prohibited women from aborting or destroying seed; a woman who does so shall be judged a murderess of children for she has caused a soul to be lost and the family of man to be diminished."

The 13th century *Zohar* taught that abortion is prohibited because "a person who kills the foetus in his wife's womb desecrates that which was built by the Holy One and His craftsmanship." It goes on to say that when Pharaoh mandated the killing of all male children, not a single Jew killed one in or out of the womb.[54]

In the New Testament, Jesus taught that human

laws have no force or validity if they contradict the rights and laws of God: "Jesus said to them, 'Render to Caesar the things that are Caesar's, and to God the things that are God's'" (Mk 12:17). Psalm 94 also condemns the unjust law of wicked tribunals: "Can wicked rulers be allied with you, who frame mischief by statute? They band together against the life of the righteous, and condemn the innocent to death" (20-21).

The meaning of all these texts as they apply to abortion is clear even in the ancient Book of Exodus: "Keep far from a false charge, and do not slay the innocent and righteous, for I will not acquit the wicked" (23:7).

The Scriptures implicitly call to task those who do nothing to fight against abortion: Proverbs 21:13 says: "He who closes his ear to the cry of the poor will himself cry out and not be heard." And Leviticus 19:16 admonishes: "Nor shall you stand by idly when your neighbor's life is at stake."*

The Scripture that speaks most of all to Christians about the horror of abortion is St. Luke's account of the Incarnation. Mary conceived in her womb by the power of the Holy Spirit. From that moment on she was pregnant with a human life possessed by the eternal Son of God who had become man. She was "with Child." Before the end of the first month, his sacred human Heart was beating beneath her heart. And his unborn relative, John, leaped for joy in his mother Elizabeth's womb when Mary carried him near.

What, the Christian must ask, does Mary think about abortion, since we are her children, members of her Son? What does Jesus, "the way, the truth, and the life" think about abortion? We must ask this question, for he said: "Take my yoke upon you, and learn from me; for I am gentle and lowly in heart, and you will find rest for your souls" (Mt 11:29). We must ask it because, as St.

Paul says, we must: "Have this mind among yourselves, which is yours in Christ Jesus, the same attitude that also Jesus Christ had" (Phil 2:5). How can we doubt what his attitude was, when we know that he came not to take life, but to give his life for the sake of our lives?

Christ bestowed the gift of the Holy Spirit on the Church, to guide her in the interpretation of these scriptural passages, so much so that he could say to Peter: "I will give you the keys of the kingdom of heaven, and whatever you bind on earth shall be bound in heaven, and whatever you loose on earth shall be loosed in heaven" (Mt 16:19).

From these texts we can see why the Church teaches that: it is a grave sin to abuse sex because it is the source of human life; it is a grave sin to abort an embryo even from the first day, because it is human life at its beginning; and it is a grave sin of murder to abort a fetus that is unmistakably a human person.

It was under the Holy Spirit's guidance concerning the meaning of these scriptural passages and of all Scripture that the Second Vatican Council called abortion and infanticide "unspeakable crimes."[55]

The Bible clearly indicates the attitude we should have toward the unborn. The golden rule Jesus gave us to guide our whole lives sums it up: "So whatever you wish that men would do to you, do so to them; for this is the law and the prophets" (Mt 7:12). This revelation from God, together with additional light from reason on the respect due human life, unmistakably shows we must reject abortion.

80

## 24. What wider consequences does the devaluing of the unborn inflict upon a society and all its members, especially the young, the old, and the hadicapped?

Abortion has so numbed consciences that they "seem dulled to the point of suffocating in each soul that inborn instinct to love and serve human life."[56] This moral numbness has led many doctors to kill for profit. It has induced legislators to subsidize killing with the excuse that it's cheaper than to support the living. It has desensitized women to the beauty of motherhood. It has eroded fatherhood by stripping away a father's right to guard the lives of his children. It has stolen parents' rights to regulate the conduct of their immature daughters. It has led couples to drift apart like falling leaves by emptying marriage of its natural meaning and consequences.

The practice of abortion has become more and more flagrant. Some mothers have babies examined in the womb, so that those with posssible birth defects can be aborted. In 1986, when Russia's Chernobyl nuclear plant disaster spewed radioactive waste over Europe, expectant mothers were worried. In Germany, Health Minister Rita Sussmunt, who was pro-abortion but concerned about the devastatingly low birth rate, assured them abortion was not called for. Still, the women flocked to abortion mills.[57]

A baby can now be examined in the womb by various tests, and treated medically. But at times the exam has other purposes. If the baby is malformed, or if it is not of the sex the parents desire, the baby is sometimes aborted. Isn't it tragic that such "choices" are hailed as the liberation of women? When one pro-choice woman politician said she thought abortion for sex choice was wrong, her political opponent charged that "her stand raised the specter of 'a state inquisitor checking with women every time they make this very difficult decision.'"[58]

In some cases medical personnel and parents allow babies who have survived abortions, and babies born malformed, to lie untreated and die.

The tissue-harvesting industry conceals a gruesome aspect of abortion. Media reports cover up the grisly details. Critics claim that the Bush Administration deprived sick people of medical help, since it would not allow the harvesting of brain cells from fetuses electively aborted. Only pro-life publications reveal the truth: "The preferred procedure for extracting brain tissue from the unborn child: 'suctioning out the brains with a plastic tube while he or she lies alive within the uterus of the mother.'" After that is done, the child is aborted.[59]

Baby destruction has robbed the sexual act of its sacredness as a source of life and love, and reduced it to a casual act of pleasure. Social conduct grows wanton in life and in the media, pornography spreads, adultery and incest multiply, and fornication, renamed premarital sex, is taken for granted.

Once children in the womb are ground up to be expelled, the ones who escape that fate are also more commonly battered after birth. Japan got off to an early start on the abortion rampage, and already years ago an article reported child abuse there. Now the same is happening in America and elsewhere.

With so many children dying, societies are greying. Watch Japan experience the effects of abortion in the coming decades. In Japan, Germany and France, young workers are growing scarce, and have to be imported.

The culture of death and the connected disintegration of families has spawned an escalating crime and murder rate. If life is not respected, what will be? Yet the obstinate demand for profligate freedom remains. The hated "criminal" today is at times the just man or

woman arrested for blocking abortion clinics. In Philadelphia a daughter wrote a letter to the editor about the
murder of her father. She complained that the man accused of his murder was a convicted felon who had shot
an officer. He was out on the streets because overcrowd-
ing had forced his release from jail. Yet at the same time,
the same prison had space to hold four pro-life demon-
strators for over four months.[60]

The demand for a higher "quality of life" has led
some to cast off anything or anyone burdensome. Eld-
erly parents may feel they are unwanted and their life is
not worthwhile. The euthanasia movement is only too
willing to agree. In California in 1992, voters cast ballots
about Proposition 161, a euthanasia initiative to legalize
assisted suicide. A year earlier, a poll commissioned by
the Hemlock Society claimed 74% support for such a
law. Proposition 161 was defeated with the help of a
vigorous campaign by the churches. Still, 45% voted in
favor.[61] The issue will arise again and again.

In the Netherlands, some doctors have practiced
assisted suicide for years. None has gone to jail, though
the practice was illegal. In February, 1993, the lower
house of the Dutch Parliament approved a law which
kept euthanasia illegal, but withheld any punishment of
doctors who followed certain requirements. One Dutch
doctor, Dr. Karel Gunning, called it murder, and said:
"Today the Netherlands abolished the Hippocratic Oath.
Killing is not part of medicine. I regret that we are becoming a barbaric nation."[62]

The only good intention we can ascribe to this law
is the legislators' desire that no one is killed without
asking to be. But that is not good enough. From a moral
point of view, abortion and euthanasia "poison human
society but they do more harm to those who practice
them than those who suffer from the injury. Moreover,
they are a supreme dishonor to the Creator."[63]

To be truly religious and moral it is not enough to be concerned only for the victims. We must be concerned for those who ask to be killed and those who kill. They face eternal judgment for their grave deeds.

Certainly, this "poison" in society gravely oppresses the handicapped. Our society does not value human beings, but their quality, like goods on a production line which discards the imperfect. How can those with serious health problems feel fully accepted? It will get worse if consciences don't awaken and cast out the death culture.

For still wider ramifications, listen to what then-Attorney General William Barr declared in 1992: "It is the breakdown of the family that is at the root of most of our social problems today." He adds: "Poverty in America—for example—is largely the result of the broken family. The incidence of poverty among two-parent families is extremely low. Almost half single-parent families are below poverty level."[64] Abortion and the attendant breakdown of sexual morality causes both the disintegration of families and the premarital sex practices that originate many of the poor single-parent families. These in turn burden the welfare system, the tax system and the whole economy.

Things are getting worse. The pill RU486 causes early abortions. In 1987 it was being marketed abroad with double-talk: "the drug's postovulatory actions may allow a retrospective decision not to become pregnant."[65] INTERPRETATION: "After you've become pregnant you can decide not to become pregnant by taking our drug." Now that abortion has become even more accepted, RU486 is being openly marketed as an easy abortion method.

What many people don't know is that contraceptive pills too often work by preventing the new life from nesting in the womb—that is, they cause abortion.

The fight against moral norms reached a new height in New York in 1993. The City Board of Education had required that AIDS education stress abstinence as the most effective way of avoiding the disease. Who could disagree? The State Commissioner of Education! He overturned the Board's decision. He couldn't deny the truth of the statement. He could only claim the Board exceeded its authority in requiring the stress on abstinence.[66]

The "new morality," which is the rejection of the eternal morality, has led to the promiscuous conduct that is generating a horde of old and new plagues, from syphilis to AIDS. A society in which these evils occur can be neither healthy nor prosperous. We have not yet seen all the forms of decay which breed and fester upon these cankers in our society.

## 25. What can we do to save the babies?

Space permits us only an overview of what we can do, in terms of our lives, prayer, work, sympathies, careers, conversations, and specific pro-life activities. Let's proceed under two headings: strategy and tactics.

STRATEGY: A strategy is an overall plan. A pro-life strategy demands familiarity with the causes and cures of the abortion syndrome. The first cause is lifestyle. As long as materialism, secularism, and rampant greed prevail, abortion will continue.

Abortion feeds on fears of overpopulation, resource scarcity and environmental pollution. These problems rise not so much from the number of people as from the greed of people. The solution lies in a simple lifestyle cleansed of consumerism, greed, and selfishness, and notable for its religious and moral standards expressed in selfless living and unselfish service. Since actions speak louder than words, our best action will be to pattern our own lives accordingly, as the Gospel invites us. Mother Teresa of Calcutta's life speaks to the world because it manifests these qualities.

Strategy requires that pro-life people work together, even when divided by issues like contraception. We can't eliminate all differences, so we admit them, and go on to concentrate on the pro-life goals we do share. Some compromise on goals and procedures (not convictions) is necessary to bring strength to the movement. In our external efforts to change government and culture, we are in the area of politics, "the art of the possible." To agree, for instance, to promote an imperfect constitutional amendment against abortion because it alone has a chance to pass is not to compromise principle. It is to act to save millions of lives by not trying at present to save every life—which might save none!

Not all have time or competence to study all the issues, but those who can should. Education and knowledge are powerful forces for good, and guide us in both strategy and tactics.

How do you change the mind and heart of a nation infected with a culture of death? "The commitment required to oppose this dramatic human condition must be expressed in a broad and organic strategy of education."[67] In this long, hard fight for truth, we won't win by demanding what is right, but by explaining what is right in season and out of season, as long as it takes to win support for pro-life legislation.

We need to sympathize with the problems of people tempted to abortion. The Holy See's *Declaration on Procured Abortion* reminds us that faithfulness to the divine law sometimes requires heroism. Some families are in crushing situations "to which in human terms there is no solution." We must understand this, be compassionate, do what we can, guided always by "the law of charity, of which the first pre-occupation must always be the establishment of justice" (nn. 24-26).

This requires that we teach morality to change attitudes, and take political action to change the law. We need to "do everything possible to help families, mothers and children" (n. 26).

Since only God converts hearts, a strategy of prayer and penance is a must. Not all pro-life people are believers, but most are. They need to recognize that without the help of the Lord of life, they'll never succeed.

We need a strategy of family support. Healthy families are the only reliable bastions of life. We should support every reasonable social program in favor of families, like the *Family and Medical Leave Act*, passed in February, 1993. In a truly human society, mothers of young children wouldn't have to work. In our culture, where many need to work, society needs to provide help to working mothers.

We need to make a religious education possible for all in our country. The interpretation of the separation of church and state that prevails today conflicts with the original intent of the writers of our Constitution. Legal and moral secularists have fabricated it. The natural law gives parents the right to educate their children according to the parents' own religious and moral convictions. Once the government taxes away parents' educational funds, it leaves them no choice but the secularist public schools. The only practical solution is to work for legislation that will provide a voucher system that enables parents to choose a school for their children.

We have stacked the deck against ourselves by calling our religious schools "private schools." In England, such schools are called public schools because they admit all who wish to come. So do most of our parochial schools. We should begin to refer to the so-called public schools as "government schools," and the rest as "citizen-run schools." That would help awaken people to the true state of things, and win new support for the voucher system.

Those who make vocation and career choices might well pray and ponder over professions such as medicine, law and politics. These offer opportunities to use one's talents not only to earn a good income, but to build the civilization of love that will abolish legal abortion.

TACTICS: What can each of us do specifically? Each one, with his or her own life situation, talents, resources and possibilities, can best answer that question with the help of the Holy Spirit. But some general directions can be stated.

We pro-life advocates are a people joined in a spiritual combat against a great evil. Each one of us needs to ponder and pray over the evil to register its magnitude and be moved to firm action. The United States lost 2,250 men at Pearl Harbor and declared war. The United States has lost over 31 million babies to abortion. These numbers are not dry statistics—they drip with blood. We must turn the pro-life campaign into a rising tide of selfless concern for human life.

We can take inspiration from campaigners like MADD (mothers against drunk driving). To stop drunk drivers seemed impossible. But campaigners have achieved so much and gotten so many laws passed that slaughter on the highways has plunged.

Ours is a spiritual war. The most effective campaign is the spiritual campaign. We wield prayer, reflection and action as our weapons for victory. Faith points to prayer as the most important of these. To win this war against death, hearts must be changed, and God is the sole Master of hearts.

Begin with a prayer now, for a particular baby in mortal danger:

> Father of life, you see a baby in the womb in danger now, for whom I want to pray, to help its mother struggling with her dread temptation. Your Son said: "Ask and you shall receive." Hear my prayer and save the child; and save the mother from the fate that could engulf her. Inspire her to say Yes! to the life in her. Give the child birth. Give it baptism in Christ, and a happy life of praise and glory to you, and such service to us all that I will have added joy in heaven when I learn of the life of this person whom you saved through my prayer. Amen.

Pray the Morning Offering each day, and add at the end, "And for the life of the unborn." Realize, when you say the Morning Offering, that your day will then become a part of the answer to your prayer. The prayer makes you a partner of Christ, a yoke-bearer with him, in bringing about the things for which you pray.

Catholics can resolve to attend Mass once a week for the babies. Say a daily Rosary to ask Mary, the new Eve, to intercede for the babies. When, in the Our Father, we pray for the coming of the civilization of love, we should hear the Father saying to us through the various teachings of Jesus: "You help us make it come."

Reflection is the second priority. Ask yourself: Who will speak out for the babies if I don't? Will I lend my voice to a baby who can't yet voice its rights?

Read to become informed. Start with the newspaper articles you see on right to life issues. Pick up the pamphlets in the back of churches, and subscribe to your diocesan paper. Collect clippings for reference.

Get a vision of what can be. The pro-life movement must tell the nation what it is for, first and foremost, rather than what it is against, just as Martin Luther King, Jr., proclaimed a vision of America that was broad enough to inspire millions of Americans. He had a dream. What is ours? Isn't it a country and a world where mothers and fathers are honored again, and where married couples are mature and disciplined enough to use and enjoy the natural rhythms of an intelligent and holy way to plan their families? Isn't it a society which orders itself by just laws, and is compassionate enough to help those who falter?

Be motivated by human and Christian principles. What human being can retain self-respect while ignoring the slaughter of innocents? What Christian can stand by while innocents are robbed of a chance for baptism into the immortal Christ? What believer or humanist can remain idle while hearing the injunction: "Nor shall you stand by idly when you neighbor's life is at stake" (Lev 19:16).*

Act today. Don't await the "Great Solution." Today is the day of salvation (cf. 2 Cor 6:2). Start with the simple things that can be done at once. Today, start a conversation about your pro-life concerns. It can awake consciences just at it can deaden them. Don't omit this. The legislator who broke the legislative tie and loosed a flood of abortions in New York State said his wife and daughter influenced him. What if they had been pro-life? Propagate the facts and the concern by word of mouth. Start at home.

Join a right to life organization. It will help you and help it. We need the power of organization. Give time and money. Little can be done without both.

Join your parish pro-life group. Begin one if necessary. Also join a national organization, to exert power at the national level. Here are several addresses: Human Life International, 7845 Airport Park, Suite E, Gaithersburgh, MD 20879; American Life Lobby, P.O. Box 490, Stafford,

VA 22555; Catholics United For Life, New Hope, KY 40052; National Right to Life Committee, Inc., 419 Seventh St., NW, Suite 500, Washington, DC 20004.

Write your national legislators in support of a human life amendment. Without it, our effectiveness will be limited. We must work toward it, no matter how long it takes. Great setbacks occurred in the anti-slavery crusade. All seemed lost. It took a terrible war but the country abolished slavery.

Vote only for pro-life politicians, even when they are less than wise in some of your other social concerns. The battle against racism triumphed when many people put it first. We can attend to lesser matters later. If we put the lesser matters first, we'll never win or deserve to win. Write your newspapers, radio and TV stations. Cull ideas for your letter from good pro-life literature. The organizations listed above send out newsletters that will provide ideas.

When you find excellent pro-life literature, ask your pastor to stock it in the church book rack, and buy copies to distribute.

Stand up for sexual morality in church and society. The biblical injunction against fornication suffers attack even in the churches. Promote natural family planning as the way to restore sound sexual morality and also provide reliable family planning. It is probably the only way to either. God and his friends in the world have providentially developed the method in our time. It is a solution staring the world in the face, and many ignore it. When married couples practice natural family planning, they find it easier to instill wholesome sexual attitudes in their children.

Support the groups that provide alternatives to pregnant women considering an abortion: counseling, emotional and financial support, housing, baby and maternity clothes, and adoption service. Your diocese may provide some of this. In 1991, the Archdiocese of Philadelphia's Catholic Social Services served 750 pregnant women with crisis pregnancies, subsidized to the amount of 1.15 million dollars, though less than half the women were Catholics. We need to give this witness.

Join people who picket abortion clinics to demonstrate and pray. Better, do sidewalk counseling of women about to enter. Learn the techniques by writing Catholics United For Life (address above). When I visited them, they introduced me to two of the lovely little girls they had rescued from abortion by sidewalk counseling. Why were they so lovely? Probably from all the love they had been given by those devoted pro-life workers! Sidewalk counseling saves lives on the spot.

Use your own station in life and your work as a basis of operation. Take to heart that we live in a finite world, and the way we live affects others. Live more simply, use less, demand less, want less, like St. Francis, the poor man of Assisi, the peacemaker. At root, it is self-centeredness and greed which kills babies. The desire for more shuts the heart and the hearth to new life, and hoards the goods that poor people need.

Do not break the sixth commandment; do not watch filthy movies or TV programs; do not tolerate pornography. They rot a society's morals. Set an example for youth. They want to be good. They lose faith in goodness without you.

In particular: fathers and mothers, devote yourselves to your family. It is the only reliable pro-life fortress because a family can fashion a home of love.

Doctors: Teach the new and effective natural family planning methods. Don't be culpably ignorant of them yourselves. Know that the Church expects much of you to promote life. The *Declaration on Procured Abortion*, asks such help for families: "Considerable progress in the service of life has been accomplished by medicine. One can hope that such progress will continue, in accordance with the vocation of doctors, which is not to suppress life but to care for it and favor it as much as possible" (n. 26).

Priests: Support the magisterium's teaching on sexuality. Be sure to carry in your bulletin notices about the natural family planning programs available in the diocese. Have NFP literature in your book rack; and include right-to-life themes in your homilies. Priests who never mention abortion, preach its acceptance by their silence (*tacere est consentire*, to be silent is to consent). Be sure to organize a right-to-life group in your parish.

Religious: Work to make the national organizations of religious heard in the right-to-life debate. Aspire to make pro-life or natural family planning a primary or at least secondary apostolate. New York's Cardinal O'Connor inspired the founding of Sisters for Life, a new congregation to do pro-life work. Anyone interested in helping or joining them can write to Sisters for Life, 198 Hollywood Ave., Bronx, NY 10465.

Highly desirable is a congregation of Sisters for Family Planning, to spread information and training for the use of natural methods of family planning. Such work will awaken consciences and heal marital morality in the Church itself. This is one of the most crucial apostolates of all.

Teachers: Assign essays and talks and run contests on pro-life topics. The book, *Know Your Body, A Family Guide to Sexuality and Fertility* by Charles W. Norris, MD, a pro-life doctor, and Jeanne Warbel Owen (Our Sunday Visitor Press) is useful to both teachers and parents. It integrates natural family planning into its reflections.

College and University faculty members: Find support and share ideas by joining University Faculty for Life, Box 2273, Georgetown University, Washington, DC 20057. Don't just talk theory, but share provocative stories that make the point. A college professor posed this problem to his students: A man with syphilis had a wife with TB. One of their children had died, and the other three suffered from incurable illnesses. What do you recommend the pregnant wife do? Answer of the students: "have an abortion." Professor: "You just killed Beethoven."

Feminists: Join Feminists for Life, P.O. Box 1539, Washington, DC 20013-1539. Their symbol, the Circle of Life, joined to the biological symbol for woman, represents "the continuum of life from conception to natural death."

Businessmen, workers, builders: create a pro-life economy and culture. Work for more economical and ample housing. Shun unfair wages and prices. You will save many lives. Your pro-life name will be written in heaven.

## Prayers for Family, Life and Love

### The Morning Offering of the Apostleship of Prayer

O Jesus, through the Immaculate Heart of Mary, I offer you my prayers, works, joys and sufferings of this day in union with the Holy Sacrifice of the Mass throughout the world. I offer them for all the intentions of your Sacred Heart: the salvation of souls, reparation for sin, the reunion of all Christians. I offer them for the intentions of our bishops and of all our members, and in particular for those recommended by our Holy Father this month, [and for the unborn]. Amen.

### Family Consecration to the Hearts of Jesus and Mary

Eternal Father, your divine Son became Man to save and restore us all. He consecrated himself for us, to assure our consecration in truth. Send your Holy Spirit to consecrate my family and all families to his Sacred Heart. Father of Life, implant in every heart such a love of life and of children that lovers of life will reclaim families and societies around the world.

Jesus our Lord, King and Center of all hearts, your Heart was the center of the Holy Family. Make it the center of every family. Make all families holy families living the truth in love.

Mindful of your promise to bless and heal families

centered in your Heart, we pray for family lives of peace and unity. Help us live by your truth in the family of your Church. We long for hearts like yours, and families living in love, sharing your mission of showing the Father's love to every human being, born and unborn.

Mary ever Virgin, Mother of Jesus, by the Eternal Father's gift you are our Queen and Mother. We consecrate ourselves to your Immaculate Heart, ever centered in Jesus' Heart. May your motherly heart, his childhood guide, inspire every mother and mother-to-be with maternal love.

St. Joseph, head of the Holy Family, instill in all families your love of the divine Heart of Jesus, and the Immaculate Heart of Mary. Train us in the family life lived in your Holy Family. When your Son was in danger, you led your family to safety. Teach us the way to safeguard the life of every child. Guide our way home to the Holy Trinity, to share with your Holy Family the life of God forever. Amen.

### A Litany to the Author of Life

*([You] "killed the Author of life, whom God raised from the dead" Acts 3:15.)*

Jesus, Author of Life, make us share your reverence for life. (The response after each petition: *Jesus, have mercy on us.*)

Jesus, eternal Son of the Father, instill in us a deep reverence for the parental role of giving life.

Jesus, sharer of our humanity from the first moment of your conception in the womb of your Virgin Mother, move us to reverence for every human life.

Jesus, formed in secret in the womb of your Virgin Mother, inspire in us a tender regard for every enwombed child.

Jesus, gestating securely in your Mother's womb, in honor of your dear Mother, the "Mother of life,"[68] move every mother to give every care to the child within her.

Jesus, guarded during your nine months in the womb by your Father in heaven and foster-father on earth, move every father to his noble task of protecting and supporting the life which is a share in his own.

Jesus, developing that Sacred Heart which began beating within your breast, beneath your Mother's Immaculate Heart, before the end of your first month in the womb, help us treasure the life of every developing child.

Jesus, saved from the depredations of Herod the child-killer by the message of an angel to Joseph, send your holy angels to inspire all of us to guard the unborn from every danger.

Jesus, Author of life, you gave your life to give us life. Inspire us to live like you in service to others, especially the unborn who are in danger of losing their lives.

Jesus, you summon us all to be born again of water and the Holy Spirit. Save all children from death in the womb. Give them a chance to be born, and to grow and respond to your call to eternal life in the Father's house. Amen.

### A Prayer for a Meeting
### of Higher Education Students for Life

**Leader:** Eternal God and Father, after the days of creation had passed, you looked at everything you had made, and found it very good. You looked with special love on young Adam and Eve. How good they were, created in the divine image and likeness!

In the new age, Jesus your Son looked with that same gaze of love on the rich young man who came in search of his future. We believe Jesus looks with love today on the young men and women here, with the riches of their own lives stretching out before them. He sees their hearts searching for the life plan that will give their days on earth full and eternal value. May he look on them with a special love because, feeling a unique solidarity with children unborn who may never have a chance to plan their lives, they have come here determined to give them that chance.

**Let us pray** (all join in):

Our Father in heaven, of all your created gifts / the most powerful is prayer's power / to call on your uncreated power. / We ask your fatherly help / in our labors of love for life. / With malice toward none / we pray for growth in knowledge and wisdom / to sort out the tangle of problems / that cost the lives of so many unborn children.

Help us bring to birth a culture / which treasures life and holds it sacred / from conception to its passage to you by earthly death.

May our way and manner of conducting ourselves / always give faithful witness / to our belief that life is a sacred trust / given by the heart of our God / and destined to return to that Heart forever.

Give us joy in the right / as expressed in the Declaration of Independence: "We hold these truths to be self-evident / that all men are created equal, / that they are endowed by their Creator / with certain unalienable rights,/ that among these are life. . . ."

Give us joy in the victory / we hope to have in your Son, who said, / "Fear not, for I have overcome the world." Amen.

## Notes

1. Vatican II, *Pastoral Constitution on the Church in the Modern World*, n. 51.

2. *Donum Vitae*, Introduction, n. 5.

3. The *Catholic League Newsletter*, August 1979, p. 3.

4. *Catholic Standard and Times*, 10/22/1992, p. 8.

5. See William P. Barr, "Affirming the American Tradition of Religious and Civil Rights," in *Catholic League Newsletter*, November, 1992, pp. 7-12.

6. "The other one without an abortion opinion," by David Boldt, *The Philadelphia Inquirer*, 9/22/91, p. 7-c.

7. The figure given in the Pennsylvania bishops' *The Church, Public Policy & Abortion* (PA Catholic Conference, April 1990).

8. See the 1982 *World Almanac*: the lists total 1,110,591 slain.

9. Quoted in *Donum Vitae*, Introduction, n. 1.

10. *Humani Generis*, n. 64; quoted in *The Teaching of the Catholic Church*, ed: Karl Rahner (Alba House, 1967), p. 31.

11. "Women trapped in abortion mill," by Frederica Mathewes-Green (*The Philadelphia Inquirer*, 3/2/90, p. 15-A).

12. *Antigone*, verses 450-460.

13. *The Philadelphia Inquirer*, 6/12/91, p. B-4.

14. John T. Noonan, Jr., *A Private Choice* (New York, The Free Press, 1979), pp. 5-6.

15. Quoted in *L'Osservatore Romano*, 12/23/76, in the article, "The Right to Life in International Documents."

16. Quoted in "Judge Kelly Innovates Rather Than Adjucates," *The Catholic Standard and Times*, 8/29/91, p. 9.

17. Quoted in *The Legal Principles of the Founding Fathers and the Supreme Court*, by Edward J. Melvin, C.M. (Pro-Life Coalition of Pennsylvania, Jenkintown, PA, undated), pp. 8-9.

18. Quoted in *The Wanderer*, 7/19/79.

19. "An Issue this Paper Can't Sidestep," *The Wall Street Journal*, 8/20/91, p. A13.

20. See article, "Birth is a Right," *The Catholic Standard and Times*, 7/1/93, p. 1, 3.

21. Vatican II, *Pastoral Constitution on the Church in the Modern World*, n. 51.

22. *California Medicine*, editorial, "A New Ethic for Law and Society" (September, 1970), p. 68.

23. "House Finds Human Life Begins at Conception," *The Wanderer*, 9/2/82.

24. See "Reflections on the Moral Status of the Pre-Embryo," *Theological Studies*, 51, 1990, pp. 603-626.

25. *The Catholic Standard and Times*, 10/24/91, p. 8.

26. *Declaration on Procured Abortion*, n. 7.

27. "When John Paul Speaks," *The Catholic Standard and Times*, 11/19/92, p. 9.

28. "Poll on Abortion Finds the Nation Sharply Divided," *New York Times*, 4/26/89, pp. A1, A25.

29. Quoted in *Declaration on Procured Abortion*, n. 6.

30. Cited in *Abortion: The Development of the Roman Catholic Perspective*, by John Connery, SJ, p. 110.

31. Germain Grisez, "When Do People Begin?" *Proceedings of the American Catholic Philosophical Association*, LXIII, pp. 27-47. Grisez gives special attention to the book, *When did I begin?*, by Norman M. Ford. Ford argues for belated individuation and animation. Grisez rejects Ford's thesis, saying that "In sum, Ford's supposedly inductive philosophical reasoning actually proceeds from judgements of common sense, based on appearances. None of his arguments show that scientists overlook philosophically significant discontinuities in development" (p. 39). Contrary to Ford, most biologists hold that individual life normally begins at fertilization.

I have read Ford's book, and do not find there convincing philosophical or biological arguments for his position.

For a far more comprehensive treatment of the abortion

issue by Grisez, see his 1993 book, *The Way of the Lord Jesus,* vol. two, *Living a Christian Life,* pp. 488-505.

32. Grisez, op. cit., 37, and footnote 49, which identifies the source of the quote: R. Yamaguchi, "Mammalian Fertilization," in *The Physiology of Reproduction,* ed. E. Knobil et al. (New York, Raven Press, 1988), p. 135.

33. Quoted in the Sacred Congregation for the Doctrine of the Faith's 1974 *Declaration on Procured Abortion,* n. 6.

34. Thomas J. O'Donnell, SJ, *Medicine and Christian Morality,* Alba House, 1976, p. 142.

35. Pastoral Constitution on the Church in the Modern World *Gaudium et Spes,* n. 51.

36. Mother Teresa said "Abortion is nothing but murder in the womb": *Philadelphia Inquirer,* 3/10/79, news brief under INTERNATIONAL: "A Nobel Prize-Winner condemns abortion."

37. For the references to *Roe v. Wade,* and an analysis of what is allowed, see Thomas J. O'Donnell, SJ, *Medicine and Christian Morality,* pp. 139-40.

38. "Abortion Conviction of Boston Doctor Upset," *New York Times,* 12/18/76, p. 1.

39. *Roe v. Wade,* in The United States LAW WEEK 41 LW 4232 (1/23/73), Justice Rehnquist, Dissenting.

40. *Ibid,* 4246.

41. Quoted in *The Fellowship of Catholic Scholars Newsletter,* December, 1992, p. 15.

42. *New York Times,* 11/10/90.

43. See the Supplement to *The Catholic League Newsletter,* vol. 12, No. 12.

44. The Couple to Couple League, P.O. Box 111184, Cincinnati, OH 45211 (513-661-7612); Billings Ovulation Method Association, The NFP Center of Washington, DC, PO Box 30239, Bethesda, MD 20824 (301-897-9323); Diocesan Development Program for NFP, 3211 Fourth St. NE, Washington, DC 20017 (202-541-3240); Pope Paul VI Institute, 6901 Mercy Rd., Omaha, NE 68106 (402-390-6600); Family of the Americas Foundation, PO Box 1170, Dunkirk, MD 20754 (301-627-3346); Northeast Family Services, 4805 N.E. Glisan St., Portland, OR 97213 (503-230-6377).

45. John T. Noonan, Jr., op. cit., pp. 190 and 192.

46. For a sobering look at over-and-under-population issues, see this author's article, "The Proliferation of population problems," *Homiletic & Pastoral Review*, February 1987, pp. 11-23.

47. Bertrand de Margerie, SJ, "Right of the unborn to eternal life threatened by abortion," *L'Osservatore Romano*, 12/8/77; reprinted (with an introductory addition by the author) in a pamphlet of the same title: Pauline Books & Media, 1979.

48. See Pius XII, Devotion to the Sacred Heart *Haurietis Aquas*, n. 130.

49. Pope John Paul II has illuminated many of these truths in his profound encyclical letter of 1980, *On the Mercy of God*. See especially n. 6 and 7.

50. See *Special Urgency of Mercy: Why Sister Faustina*, by George W. Kosicki, C.S.B. (Franciscan University Press, Steubenville, 1990) pp. 31, 41, etc.

51. John Connery, S.J., *Abortion: The Development of the Roman Catholic Perspective*, pp. 12, 21. See chapter one, pp. 1-21.

52. "Catechism's Hot List of New Sins for the '90s," *National Jesuit News*, February, 1993, p. 6.

53. "The Hippocratic Oath," quoted in *L'Osservatore Romano*, 5/11/78, p. 10. In some universities where the Hippocratic oath is read at medical school graduations, the line about abortion is now dropped!

54. "Abortion," *Encyclopedia Judaica*.

55. Vatican II, *Pastoral Constitution on the Church in the Modern World*, n. 51.

56. "In the Service of Life," III (The Pontifical Council for the Family, Vatican City, 1991).

57. Human Life International, Special Report, n. 22, 11/17/79, p. 6.

58. "Abortion Issue Taking Odd Turn in California," The *New York Times*, 5/15/90, p. A22.

59. "Grim Harvest," The *Catholic World Report*, August 1992, pp. 16-22.

60. *Catholic Standard and Times*, 1/7/93, p. 7.

61. "Proposition 161 Defeated," *Life at Risk*, NCCB Secretariat for Pro-Life Activities, November 1992.

62. "Dutch Parliament Approves Law Permitting Euthanasia," *New York Times*, 2/10/93, p. A10.

63. Vatican II, *Gaudium et Spes*, 27.

64. "Affirming the American Tradition of Religious and Civil Rights," *Catholic League Newsletter*, November 1992, p. 10.

65. "Medical Double-Talk on Abortion," *The Medical Moral Newsletter*, January 1987, p. 1.

66. "New York State Overturns Rule on AIDS Study," *New York Times*, 2/9/93, p. A1.

67. "In the Service of Life," III (cited above).

68. "Mother of life" is a title given to Mary by Pope John Paul II in his 10/7/79 homily in our nation's Capitol. Published in U.S.A., *The Message of Justice, Peace and Love*, by John Paul II (Pauline Books & Media, 1979), p. 286.

# St. Paul Book & Media Centers

**ALASKA**
750 West 5th Ave., Anchorage, AK 99501; 907-272-8183

**CALIFORNIA**
3908 Sepulveda Blvd., Culver City, CA 90230; 310-397-8676
5945 Balboa Ave., San Diego, CA 92111; 619-565-9181
46 Geary Street, San Francisco, CA 94108; 415-781-5180

**FLORIDA**
145 S.W. 107th Ave., Miami, FL 33174; 305-559-6715

**HAWAII**
1143 Bishop Street, Honolulu, HI 96813; 808-521-2731

**ILLINOIS**
172 North Michigan Ave., Chicago, IL 60601; 312-346-4228

**LOUISIANA**
4403 Veterans Memorial Blvd., Metairie, LA 70006; 504-887-7631

**MASSACHUSETTS**
50 St. Paul's Ave., Jamaica Plain, Boston, MA 02130; 617-522-8911
Rte. 1, 885 Providence Hwy., Dedham, MA 02026; 617-326-5385

**MISSOURI**
9804 Watson Rd., St. Louis, MO 63126; 314-965-3512

**NEW JERSEY**
561 U.S. Route 1, Wick Plaza, Edison, NJ 08817; 908-572-1200

**NEW YORK**
150 East 52nd Street, New York, NY 10022; 212-754-1110
78 Fort Place, Staten Island, NY 10301; 718-447-5071

**OHIO**
2105 Ontario Street, Cleveland, OH 44115; 216-621-9427

**PENNSYLVANIA**
510 Holstein Street, Bridgeport, PA 19405; 215-277-7728

**SOUTH CAROLINA**
243 King Street, Charleston, SC 29401; 803-577-0175

**TENNESSEE**
4811 Poplar Ave., Memphis, TN 38117; 901-761-0874

**TEXAS**
114 Main Plaza, San Antonio, TX 78205; 210-224-8101

**VIRGINIA**
1025 King Street, Alexandria, VA 22314; 703-549-3806

**GUAM**
285 Farenholt Avenue, Suite 308, Tamuning, Guam 96911; 671-649-4377

**CANADA**
3022 Dufferin Street, Toronto, Ontario, Canada M6B 3T5; 416-781-9131